CLIMBING *The World's Best Sites*

CLIMBING
The World's Best Sites

GARTH HATTINGH

NEW YORK

First published in the
United States of America in 1999 by
RIZZOLI INTERNATIONAL PUBLICATIONS, INC.
300 Park Avenue South, New York, NY 10010

First published in Great Britain in 1999
by New Holland Publishers (UK) Ltd
London • Cape Town • Sydney • Auckland

ISBN 0-8478-2226-5
LC 99-70263

DESIGNER **PETER BOSMAN**
EDITOR **THEA GROBBELAAR**
PUBLISHING MANAGER **MARIËLLE RENSSEN**
ILLUSTRATOR **DANIËL JANSEN VAN VUUREN**
PICTURE RESEARCHER **CARMEN WATTS**
CONSULTANTS **JON TINKER (UK)** AND
GREG PRITCHARD (AUSTRALIA)
PROOFREADER AND INDEXER **SEAN FRASER**

Reproduction by
HIRT & CARTER (PTY) LTD, CAPE TOWN
Printed and bound in Singapore by
TIEN WAH PRESS (PTE) LTD

BEAUFORT SEA

GREENLAND

BAFFIN BAY

NORWEGIAN

▲ Polar Sun Spire

ICELAND

ALASKA

▲ Mount McKinley

Anchorage ○   ▲ Mount Logan

UNITED
KINGDOM

Ben Nevis ▲

Clogwyn Du'r Arddu
Dinas Chromlech   ▲
                   London

HUDSON
BAY

CANADA

Vancouver ○

UNITED STATES OF AMERICA

Montreal

El Capitan

▲ Long's Peak
The Diamond

Washington DC ○   ○ New York

PACIFIC

**Super
Crack**

▲   ▲

The Naked Edge

ATLANTIC

Madrid

PORTUGAL SPAIN

MOROCCO

Tropic of Cancer

MEXICO

CUBA

MAURITANIA

COSTA RICA

VENEZUELA

SENEGAL   MALI

SIERRA LEONE

COLOMBIA

Equator

ECUADOR ▲

Chimborazo

PERU

Lima ○

BRAZIL

Illampu ▲

OCEAN

BOLIVIA

OCEAN

PARAGUAY

Rio de Janeiro

Tropic of Capricorn

Llullaillaco ▲

CHILE

URUGUAY

Santiago ○   ▲ *Aconcagua*

ARGENTINA

N

▲ *Cerro Torre*

▲
*Cerro San
Valentin*

SOUTH

ARCTIC OCEAN

EAST SIBERIAN SEA

BARENTS SEA

SEA

SWEDEN
FINLAND

NORWAY

RUSSIAN FEDERATION

SEA OF
OKHOTSK

BERING SEA

DENMARK

Moscow

*Action
Directe*

BELARUS

Matterhorn

Open Air

UKRAINE

Eiger

KAZAKHSTAN

MONGOLIA

Paris

HUNGARY

*Mont
Blanc*

ROMANIA

Beijing

JAPAN

ITALY
Rome

Istanbul

Elbrus

*Gasherbrum 2
Gasherbrum*

▲ *Mount Fuji*

TURKEY

The Ogre

K2

Algiers

*Mount
Olympus*

GREECE

Tehran

IRAQ

AFGHANISTAN

Nanga Parbat

CHINA

PACIFIC

IRAN

Dhaulagiri

Annapurna

Cairo

PAKISTAN

Delhi

Everest

LIBYA

EGYPT

SAUDI
ARABIA

NEPAL

Karachi

TAIWAN

ALGERIA

INDIA

NIGER

CHAD

SUDAN

YEMEN

BURMA

Khartoum

Bangkok

PHILIPPINES

NIGERIA

THAILAND

Lagos

ETHIOPIA

SRI
LANKA

OCEAN

MALAYSIA

KENYA

Mount Kenya

PAPUA NEW
GUINEA

ZAIRE

Nairobi

INDIAN

INDONESIA

Kilimanjaro

TANZANIA

ANGOLA

ZAMBIA

CORAL SEA

ZIMBABWE

NAMIBIA

MADAGASCAR

AUSTRALIA

OCEAN

SOUTH
AFRICA

Cape Town

*Table
Mountain*

Ozymandias

Sydney

The Bard ▲

▲

ERN OCEAN

*Ball's
Pyramid*

Mount Cook ▲

Wellington

NEW
ZEALAND

What can be said to constitute a 'top' climb? As interpreted in this volume, a top or great climb can be an 8000m (26,000ft) peak, or an ice waterfall; it can be a short but devastatingly difficult route up an overhanging cliff next to a highway; it can be in Antarctica or the Himalayas, or in small local hills. What all these disparate routes share is the consensus among a significant number of climbers that the climb is an unforgettable experience in its particular branch of the sport, a classic of its type. As is the case with good books and music, some classics are only a year or two old; some go back well over two centuries. An elusive blend of history, setting, location, atmosphere, difficulty and aesthetics make a route 'great'. An attempt has been made in this book to identify a selection of climbs ranging across the full spectrum of climbing which, for varying reasons, are special, memorable, stupendous routes (a route in climbing jargon being a way up a peak or mountain, a cliff or ice waterfall – a complete climb, of whatever length).

Certain peaks virtually select themselves – such as Mount Everest, K2, the Eiger and the Matterhorn. These are household names, and each has an irrefutable place in the history and development of mountaineering. Other climbs selected are more open to debate.

The specific route that has been emphasized is not always that of the first climbers to ascend the peak. Often, subsequent routes are deemed by the climbing fraternity to be more elegant (an elegant route in climbing terms is one which takes an aesthetically or technically pleasing 'line' to the summit). All of these climbs, be they the first ascent of the peak or not, were in their day or are presently still considered to be the most logical or most challenging routes on the peak in question.

It is in the nature of things that many will disagree with the final selection of routes, and the author in all humility acknowledges that the selection of one route above another is purely subjective. Longer routes and high mountains tend to require more attempts before a route is completed, and thus have a richer history than shorter, lower climbs. There are thus more high peaks and

Above The renowned Sherpa, Tenzing Norgay, at an Everest reunion in 1973.

Left Reinhold Messner, illustrious South Tyrolean mountaineer, at K2 Base Camp.

Top left The late Rob Hall on the summit of Mount Everest, the first of his five ascents of the peak.

'big walls' than short rock or sport climbs – indeed the latter are included merely to give a taste of what these branches of the sport are about.

Great climbs could not be achieved without great climbers, and the book owes its existence to the lives and exploits of those who were (or may still be) at the forefront of the activity – thank you all! In many cases, the ascent of the route has been accompanied by a good deal of drama, and even death. The nature of climbing at the cutting edge of the sport, which is where a great many of these routes lay when first climbed, or where they may still lie, is like any extreme activity – open to danger. The intention of the book is, however, not to give vicarious pleasure to the bloodthirsty but rather to tell the stories of pleasure, of heroism, of courage, of determination. Record is given of the triumphs and joy of

218BC	1492	<1500	1642	1786	1834
ALPS	MONT AIGUILLE	LLULLAILLACO	MT WASHINGTON	MONT BLANC	MONT AIGUILLE
Italy	2097m (6880ft)	6723m (22,057ft)	1916m (6288ft)	4807m (15,771ft)	2097m (6880ft)
Hannibal, with 37	France-Dauphine	Chilean Andes	Rockies, USA	France-Italy	France-Dauphine
elephants, 9000 men	De Ville and 10 men,	Atacama Indians	Field and two	Paccard, Balmat	Young shepherd boy
	by order of Charles VIII		Amerindians		looking for lost goats!

Right The setting sun imparts dramatic colour to the Southwest Face of Mount Everest.

first ascensionists, and the fun and games that often accompanied the exploits of these enthusiastic climbers, who were frequently dynamic young men and women bursting with vitality and ambition. Sadly, also written into the stone, the ice and the snow are many tragic episodes, when the unforgiving nature of climbing overcame the best efforts of the pioneers. These are the climbers, often in the prime of their life, whom we must remember proudly, not mournfully, for they opened the way for others. Their efforts helped to redefine the limits of human endeavour and courage; their sacrifices came about knowingly, in pursuit of their passion, their dream, for many their entire motivation in life. Those who are recorded here as dying in the mountains or hills were neither foolish nor wasteful of their lives. Unfortunate, perhaps; careless, perhaps. But they were not silly, spoilt youngsters who should have known better, who should have stayed at home and watched the football game on television. They are the folk heroes who lift us out of our everyday lives, whose exploits we marvel at. Their tragedy is our tragedy. We cannot identify with our climbing heroes, puffing up our chests and sharing their triumphs, without also being prepared to share their failures, their disappointments, their final tragic moments.

Both climbers and nonclimbers frequently ask 'Why climb?'

Perhaps, 'Because it's there,' to quote George Mallory? Nicholas O'Connel, in his superb book, *Beyond Risk – Conversations with Climbers*, has interviewed many of the world's leading climbers, and obtained some answers to this question. They display a wealth of motivation. Climbing is lifted

out of the realm of 'mere adventure' into an almost spiritual dimension by the philosophies of these people, whose ranks include the most accomplished climbers in the world.

Out of O'Connel's interviews emerge some of the motivations of these famous climbers – the escape from the drudgery of everyday life, the love of the outdoors and its beauty and grandeur, the appreciation of comradeship that can only come to fullness under extreme duress, a curiosity and wonder about what lies over the horizon, a thirst for adrenaline, a route to self-discovery, or climbing 'just for the heck of it'. Whatever the mixed motivations, the exploits of these pioneers give a rich and varied mosaic of the sport of climbing, showing it as it is for many climbers – a way of life, rather than a casual leisure activity. On their feats we can slake our thirst for adventure.

One soon realizes that climbers do not have a 'death wish'. One of the greatest living climbers, Reinhold Messner, summed up his attitude as such: 'Without danger of death, climbing is no longer climbing. I'm not seeking death on the climb – exactly the opposite – I'm trying to survive. But it's very easy to survive if there's no danger of death. Climbing is the art of surviving in very difficult situations that involve the danger of death. And the best climber is not the one who does a crazy thing once or twice and dies the second time; the best climber is one who does many things on the highest level and survives.'

He goes on to say, 'You should know "this I can do, and this I cannot do". This is one of the basic parts of climbing, to know in every second, "This is my limit. I cannot go above it. I should stay a little below." And if you go above too many

1857	1865	1868	1874	1881	1887
(British) Alpine Club formed	MATTERHORN 4477m (14,690ft) Switzerland Whymper party	LONG'S PEAK 4344m (14,255ft) Colorado, USA Powell, Byers	Club Alpin Français formed	Mummery and party first use wooden wedges for aid	Winkler first uses iron claws (primitive crampons)

Left Machapuchare, also known as Fishtail Mountain, as seen from the Annapurna Sanctuary.

to complete the picture – and the shortest, boldest pieces of thread can often be the most essential to the beauty of the finished work. 'I would rather burn briefly with a bright flame that illuminates man's glory, than linger dully forever, shedding no light on anything.'

This book is penned in deep appreciation of all those whose names feature in it, and to the many other unsung 'Greats' who enrich the climbing tapestry for the pleasure of all who care to gaze on it or perhaps even dare to add their own small thread to the weave.

A BRIEF HISTORY OF MOUNTAINEERING

Mountains have always held an appeal for mankind. It is often the unattainability of the peaks that give them their pre-eminence, or their beauty.

From the earliest accounts, you find mountains associated with the great religions of man, with the philosophers, artists, sages and scientists. Many peaks are still held as sacred, with the actual summits being 'off limits', such as Kanchengjunga, 8586m (28,170ft); Machapuchare, 6993m (23,000ft); and Kailas, 6700m (22,000ft), which is regarded as the Throne of Shiva and the very centre of Buddhist and Hindu worship. North American Indians still hold desert spires sacred as ancestral holy places. This mystical-religious theme echoes throughout the mountains of the world – Mount Olympus, the home of the Greek gods; Mount Kenya, the place of the spirits of the Kikuyu; Mount Fuji, again an ancestral spirit home. People's reactions to mountains have undergone vast changes – as late as 1690, the Bishop of Geneva undertook a 'journey of mortal peril' to exorcise the glaciers of Chamonix, which

times, you will surely die climbing. And the art of climbing is surviving, not dying.'

Coming from one of the most successful and influential alpine and high-altitude climbers of the modern age, these are salutary words indeed. Messner, in striving to conquer all the 8000m (26,000ft) peaks, set the standards by which future climbs will be judged for many years – solo ascents of major peaks without oxygen; fast, free alpine-style climbs; harder and harder variation routes. His climbs, on closer inspection, do not show a lunatic foolhardiness, but a precisely evaluated, carefully executed boldness. And so it was with most of the great climbers, the hard-driving pioneers. They were not shallow adventurers or mere fame seekers. They were visionaries in their own right – bold yet prudent, tough yet philosophical in their attitude and approach to the mountains,

desirous of enriching and perfecting their lives through the tempering experiences of climbing.

In climbing, one can pack the normal human experiences of weeks, months or years into the ambit of a few tightly focused minutes, a few hours, or a few days. Perhaps it is this intensity which entices and motivates climbers. And this finely distilled essence, rich in flavour and experience, is savoured by all who live it or read about it, making mountaineering stories irresistible to even those who ascend nothing more ambitious than their office stairs. The desperate and fruitless attempts to save Toni Kurz on the Eiger, Reinhold Messner's frantic search for his brother on Nanga Parbat, the exultation of Maurice Herzog on Annapurna, Catherine Destivelle's bold solo of the Dru – all are rich threads in the tapestry of climbing. They add their pattern to the weave, helping

1889	1894	1897	1899	1910	1913
KILIMANJARO	MT COOK	ACONCAGUA	MT KENYA	MT McKINLEY (N)	MT McKINLEY (S)
5895m (19,341ft)	3754m (12,316ft)	6962m (22,840ft)	5199m (17,058ft)	5934m (19,469ft)	6193m (20,319ft)
Kenya/Tanzania	New Zealand	Argentina	Kenya	Alaska, USA	Alaska, USA
Meyer, Purtscheller	Graham, Fyfe, Clark	Zurbriggen solo	McKinder, Hausberg	Anderson, Taylor	Stuck, Karstens
	(only 17 years old)			(Sourdough)	

Above Mont Blanc, with its covering of snow, is the highest point in the European Alps.

Right Good jamming technique is essential for the roof crack on Passport to Insanity, Grampians.

Top right A rescue helicopter prepares to lift an injured climber from the summit of the Eiger.

as 'the worke of the deville were crushinge the barns'. It is perhaps hard for us to imagine the superstitious fear with which our ancestors regarded these inaccessible peaks, yet the Tibetans and other mountain people still hold very similar beliefs today.

Many ascended mountains, as did Moses, with a religious motive. Other motives have been more obscure, or more dubious. One interesting motive was that of Dompjulien de Beaupré, Chamberlain to Charles VIII of France, who was ordered (in no uncertain terms) to ascend Mont Aiguille (2097m; 6880ft) just south of Grenoble in 1492. Many before him had attempted this steep-walled, imposing spire only to die or be beaten back, cowed and humble. De Beaupré was not so easily defeated, and laid siege to the mountain with ladders and ropes, accompanied by a number of no doubt terrified soldiers. He eventually succeeded, but could find no trace of the angels reputed to float on top of this admittedly exquisite peak, only (amazingly!) a herd of chamois on the large, flat top. The peak was not ascended again until 1834, which gives us some idea of the magnitude of his accomplishment.

One might be tempted to wonder why it took so long to get up a route or peak that is now considered 'easy' – a classic example might be the *voie normale* on Mont Blanc, now ascended by hundreds every single day in high season. The psychological disadvantage of being the first must never be discounted, neither must the difficulties of route finding, or the primitive nature of the equipment and climbing techniques which constituted the entire armoury of the early pioneers. A superb example is that of cracks which were once considered 'impossible' to negotiate now being ascended fluidly using the 'Dülfer technique', an opposed-pressure lay-back which the Bavarian Hans Dülfer pioneered in the early 1900s, or via the inimitable 'hand jams' of the British climber Joe Brown. Things are often much easier for the second party. That great British climber, Alfred Mummery, talking of the then-notorious Grepon, humorously described the progress in climbing as 'an inaccessible peak – the most difficult climb in the Alps – an easy day for a lady' – not far off the truth in that particular case. On the other side of the coin, Heinrich Harrer, author of *The White Spider* and one of the German opening party on the North Face of the Eiger, talking about the unpredictable and vicious nature of that great face, said with some accuracy, '...In this sense, every ascent of the Eiger North Face will always be a first ascent.' Some climbs simply never get easier or safer for subsequent parties.

The Western World would probably credit the first ascent of Mont Blanc in 1786 by two local Chamonix climbers, Michel Paccard, a scientist, and Jacques Balmat, a crystal hunter, as the birth of 'true mountaineering'. This was a feat of great courage, and opened the path for the exploration of the high peaks of the world.

1924	1928	1938	1950	1952	1953
Mallory and Irvine lost on Everest	Himalayan Club founded	EIGER 3970m (13,024ft) Switzerland Heckmair, Vörg, Harrer, Kasparek	ANNAPURNA 8091m (26,545ft) Nepal Herzog, Lachenal	FITZROY 3405m (11,170ft) Patagonia Terray, Magnone	EVEREST 8848m (29,028ft) Nepal Hillary, Norgay

Above Al Stevenson and Ian Howell on the summit of Rani Peak.

Left Great precision is required for friction slab climbing in the Yosemite Valley, California.

The time between the formation of the Alpine Club in Britain in 1857 and the epic disaster on the Matterhorn – the famous Whymper saga of 1865 – was referred to as the Golden Age of Alpine mountaineering, during which over 200 great peaks of Europe were climbed, largely by British mountaineers with their Alpine guides. It was only when the 'eccentric diversion' became a popular pastime for the British gentry of the late 1800s that the 'sport' of mountaineering was truly born. For years before this, 'scientific studies' were used as a thinly veiled excuse for mountaineering.

Soon significant ascents were being made of already climbed peaks by new and more difficult routes – climbing was being done for climbing's sake alone, without the need for further justification. The Brenva Ridge of Mont Blanc and the numerous first climbs of Alfred Mummery were the first in a series of 'great variation routes'. Marie Paradis, a French villager, made the first female ascent of Mont Blanc in 1808. Women were increasingly being drawn to the peaks.

The rest of the world was soon in line behind the British, with Americans such as the Reverend William Coolidge, who climbed 600 Alpine grand courses or big climbs with his aunt and his dog for company! The 1900s saw a phenomenal amount of climbing until World War I interrupted things, with outstanding routes opened in the early 1900s by climbers such as the Englishmen Geoffrey Winthrop-Young and George Mallory, the brilliant Frenchman Armand Charlet, and of course the famous Swiss guide, Josef Knubel. Fine climbs were regularly being opened in many countries throughout the world, despite the fact that climbers were still generally regarded as 'lunatics.'

In America, Colorado had already been identified as a great area – the crossroads of American climbing. The Rockies sweep suddenly upwards out of the plains, a great tidal wave of geological upheaval, with a full range of rock climbing on offer, from bouldering to alpine-style climbing and big wall routes. The concept of climbing more difficult routes 'just for the heck of it' emerged, and the Boulder area in particular, with Hallet Peak, Estes Peak, and Long's Peak (called 'The American Matterhorn') with its incomparable East Face, became a focal point of effort with many high-standard routes being opened.

In the Yosemite Valley, California, legendary American climbers such as Yvon Chouinard, Layton Kor and Royal Robbins pushed standards of climbing even higher. The great walls of Yosemite, which are still held in awe, were the test pieces of the day.

Early climbers in America included some interesting characters, such as those who took part in the famous Sourdough ascent of Mount McKinley in Alaska (6193m; 20,319ft). A group of tough, hardened miners decided to climb this, one of the highest peaks in North America, simply

for the fun of it, and succeeded, albeit they had an exceedingly hard time convincing anyone of the truthfulness of their claim.

It was, however, the European Alps, with their fascinating and intricately interwoven rock and ice walls and spires, which were, and still are, considered to be the real proving ground for climbers. Milestone routes included those of the Italian, Riccardo Cassin, with his amazing ascent of the notorious Walker Spur in 1938, and the spine-chilling first ascent of the Eiger by Austrians Kasparek and Harrer, and Germans Heckmair and Vörg in the same year. Somewhat later another Italian, Walter Bonatti, made climbing history with his six-day solo ascent of the Petit Dru in 1955, and his epic descent of the multi-pinnacled Flammes de Pierre. All these were outstanding climbs, well ahead of their time. The Americans, too, made some notable ascents of the European Alps in the 1950s and 1960s. Climbers such as John Harlin, Guy Hemmings and Royal Robbins pioneered futuristic routes like the American

1953	1954	1955	1958	1959	1970
NANGA PARBAT	K2	PETIT DRU	EL CAPITAN	CERRO TORRE	CERRO TORRE
8125m (26,658ft)	8611m (28,253ft)	3733m (12,248ft)	2305m (7562ft)	3133m (10,280ft)	3133m (10,280ft)
Pakistan	Pakistan	France	Yosemite, USA	Patagonia	Patagonia
Buhl solo	Lacedelli. Compagnoni	Bonatti	Harding, Merry, Whitmore (37 days)	Maestri, Egger (disputed)	Maestri (the infamous 'bolt ladder')

Above Catherine Destivelle perches precariously on the sheer face of Devil's Tower in Wyoming.

Right The unmistakable peak of the majestic Matterhorn as seen from Zermatt.

with the Himalayas recently being referred to as the 'super Alps'. Oxygenless ascents, one-day alpine-style pushes, winter routes, harder and harder variants are now a part of the Himalayan game, with faster and more daring attempts of necessity replacing the creation of new routes.

South America, in particular Patagonia, southern Chile and Argentina, attracted the strong climbers, and the easily accessible peaks of Peru and Bolivia drew the rest. Many new, bold lines were made, including the Italian guide Cesare Maestri's controversial 'bolt ladder' up Cerro Torre.

Modern targets are the frozen, windswept mountains of Antarctica and Patagonia, and those of the Canadian hinterland. Remoteness and difficult access make these worthy challenges, and it will probably be many decades before every peak has seen an ascent. There are still many virgin peaks below 7000m (23,000ft) in the Himalayas, and untouched rock faces scattered all over the world. It is somehow comforting to know that for the pioneering climber, there are still many challenges waiting.

THE CLIMBING GAME

Lito Tejada-Flores, in his landmark essay *Games Climbers Play*, clearly spells out the 'gaming' element inherent in climbing. In the end, with climbing no longer having the credibility of being a 'scientific endeavour', what else is it but a sport, a game? And games must have rules and mores.

To ascend a rock face solo with no equipment is undoubtedly the purest form of the game. Any gear starts to alter the chances of success or survival. For instance, to ascend a normal, easy, alpine rock route using fixed ropes, ladders and drilled bolts for aid makes the whole exercise ludicrous; to do the same route using standard climbing gear places the exercise within 'acceptable rules of play'. An element of uncertainty in

Direct on the Dru. Not to be outdone, the British retaliated with the successful attempt by Chris Bonington, Ian Clough, Don Whillans and Jan Dlugosz (Polish) on the challenging Central Pillar of Frêney in 1961. Alpine climbing standards were slowly forced ever upwards.

As the playgrounds of Europe and America succumbed to the onslaught of increasing numbers in the early 1900s, the leading climbers started to turn to some of the other grand mountain ranges of the world. Climbers fixed their eyes on the 8000m (26,000ft) peaks, and of course, prime among them, Mount Everest. In the 1920s the British in particular started to spiral in on Everest, also known as Chomolungma, or the Mother Goddess of the Earth, but it was only after numerous unsuccessful but often close attempts that New Zealander Edmund Hillary and Sherpa Tenzing Norgay finally stood on the summit in 1953.

Thereafter, expedition followed expedition to the Himalayas until all of the 8000m peaks had been climbed. Then the 'variation' routes began,

the outcome of any climb is the ultimate goal of the true adventure climber, and the rules of the game are set to match. To a certain extent, the mountain must have a chance!

This element of risk is always greater for those on the pioneering ascents, as they are entering arenas where the boundaries are unknown, the nature of the experience uncertain, the target unclear. Subsequent ascents are often easier, although this may well be a relative term, as weather, conditions of the route and many other imponderables can lead to subsequent attempts being more arduous than the original. You only need to examine the lives lost in the mountains each year on repeats of routes to recognize this.

Just as a golfer may play simply for fun at a local course, or for huge money in international events, so a climber may select smaller stakes, as in a short, easy sport route that makes no real demands, or he or she may choose to go for a gamble of monumental proportions, such as a solo, in winter, on an unclimbed Himalayan peak.

1970	1978	1979	1991	1992	1993
NANGA PARBAT	EVEREST	Ray Jardine invents	PETIT DRU	EIGER	EL CAPITAN
8125m (26,658ft)	8848m (29,028ft)	'Friends' – camming	3733m (12,248ft)	3970m (13,026ft)	2305m (7562ft)
Pakistan	Nepal	protection devices	France	Switzerland	Yosemite, USA
Messner brothers	Reinhold Messner,		Destivelle	Destivelle	Hill, Sandahl (free
	Habeler (sans oxygen)				at Grade 5.13b)

THE 8000M PEAKS

THE 8000M PEAKS

MOUNT EVEREST • ANNAPURNA • K2 • NANGA PARBAT

The 8000m (26,000ft) peaks eluded climbers until the 1950s, the combination of altitude, weather and technical difficulty accounting for the deaths of many climbers. Although Mount Everest has the highest number of deaths of any of these peaks, relative to the large numbers of climbers who attempt or ascend Everest, it does not lay claim to the highest death rate. This doubtful privilege must be shared between K2 and Nanga Parbat.

K2 (8611m; 28,253ft) has a macabre and well-deserved reputation as a killer peak. It is both technically difficult, having no 'easy' line, and subjectively difficult, with constant storm and avalanche danger. Add to this a 190km (120-mile) walk-in, and it is hardly surprising that K2 sees fewer attempts than most of the other 8000m peaks. In 1939, Dudley Wolfe (USA) and three Sherpas died in a storm; Art Gilkey (USA) was killed in 1953 after the whole team fell while attempting to take him down, and a year later Mario Puchoz (Italy) succumbed to pulmonary oedema. Nick Estcourt (UK) fell to his death on the West Ridge in 1978, and in 1986, a total of 13 climbers died – although admittedly 10 teams reached the top (eight via the Abruzzi Ridge). K2 still takes its toll, numbering among its recent fatalities the avalanche deaths of American Dan Culver and the UK's Allison Hargreaves, while Spaniard Atxo Apellaniz died of exposure and exhaustion.

Nanga Parbat (8125m; 26,658ft) became known as the 'German Mountain', because of the focus of interest by Dr Karl Herrligkoffer – in much the same way as Everest was the 'British Mountain', Annapurna the 'French Mountain', and K2 the 'Italian Mountain'. The Germans were to pay dearly for their prize – 10 climbers died in 1934, and another 16 in 1937. Before that, during the 1895 expedition, two Gurkhas had perished along with the indomitable Alfred Mummery. In 1950 two British climbers, Thornley and Crace, were killed, and in 1963 Sigi Löw, returning from the summit, slipped in a 'harmless' gully near the base and fell to his death. In 1970 Reinhold Messner's brother, Günther, lost his life in an avalanche while descending from their successful ascent of the Rupal Face.

In just over 100 years, more than 40 climbers, half of them Sherpas, have died on Nanga Parbat. The malevolent nature of the mountain indeed became apparent long before the first climbers attempted to conquer it – in the mid-19th century a huge rock slide from Nanga Parbat dammed the Indus River, creating a huge lake. This natural dam later broke, and the resulting flood decimated an entire Sikh army, as well as killing hundreds of people lower down in the plains.

Perhaps 'killer peaks' can be put into their true perspective by Reinhold Messner, who said: 'It is nonsense to talk of the curse of Nanga Parbat … it is simply because it is so much bigger than we mere mortals.' (From *Games Climbers Play.*)

Although only a few peaks have been discussed here in some detail, all 14 of the 8000m peaks (*see* page 158) represent serious mountaineering, and most of them have stories of great heroism or drama attached. All the world's peaks over 8000m are situated in the Himalayas – the name is derived from the Sanskrit terms *hima* (snow) and *alaya* (abode) – the immense 2400km (1500-mile) zone of high mountains stretching across the Asian continent. Included in this area are also over 400 peaks which exceed 7000m (23,000 ft), many of which are just as difficult in their own right as their 'magic 8000m' brethren.

MOUNT EVEREST
Location: Nepal Himalayas
Summit height: 8848m (29,028ft)
First ascent: South Col – Edmund Hillary, Tenzing Norgay, leader John Hunt (UK), 29 May 1953

ANNAPURNA
Location: Nepal Himalayas
Summit height: 8091m (26,545ft)
First ascent: North Face – Maurice Herzog and Louis Lachenal (France), 3 June 1950

K2
Location: Central Karakoram
Summit height: 8611m (28,253ft)
First ascent: Abruzzi Ridge – Lino Lacedelli and Achille Compagnoni (Italy), 31 July 1954

NANGA PARBAT
Location: Punjab Himalayas
Summit height: 8125m (26,658ft)
First ascent: Rakhiot Face – Hermann Buhl, solo, 3 July 1953

Previous pages Two climbers from the 1997 South African Everest expedition head off from a high camp.
Opposite Nanga Parbat's impressive 3350m (11,000ft) North (Rakhiot) Face, seen from Fairy Meadows.
Top right Memorial to dead climbers, K2 Base Camp, Karakoram – a sobering reminder of one's mortality.

Mount Everest

The Top of the World — Conquering the Giant

In 1856, the British surveyor general in India, Andrew Waugh, established that 'Peak XV', at 8848m (29,028ft), was the highest in the known world. He decided to name the peak 'Everest' in honour of his respected predecessor, George Everest. The Tibetan name, Chomolungma or 'Goddess Mother of the Earth', was used locally, and Everest himself protested that local inhabitants could not pronounce the 'new' name, nor could it be written in Hindi. Nonetheless, it has prevailed as the household name. It soon became the target of many nations and mountaineers. It is in the nature of mankind that superlatives spur the greatest efforts. The 'highest mountain in the world' is like a flame to a moth – sadly, often with similar results.

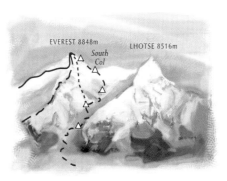

- - Hillary 1953   — — West Ridge 1979
.... Southwest Face 1975   —— Messner Solo 1980

Francis Younghusband (UK) pioneered the way into Tibet in 1903, and after covering a distance of 100km (62 miles) brought the news that the North Ridge offered a probable path. In 1913, the adventurer, Captain John Noel (UK), made an illicit foray into Tibet, his hair and skin artificially darkened so that he could pass as a native of the region. A full expedition was postponed until 1921 because of the unstable political situation in Tibet and Nepal, and the various wars around the turn of the century which culminated in World War I. The Royal Geographical Society and the (British) Alpine Club formed the Everest Committee after a strong motivational lecture from Noel, and the result was the 1921 British expedition, led by Lt Col Charles Howard-Bury, and including George Mallory. Mallory was a passionate mountaineer, and it became his ambition to ascend Everest. The expedition disintegrated as a result of politics and altitude problems, but not before Mallory and his companions had penetrated the Rongbuk Glacier to a point overlooking the Western Cwm (pronounced 'Coombe') in Nepal. Mallory commented that this western side looked favourable, and indeed he was proved correct, as many years later the first ascent followed this route. A later reconnaissance on the same expedition led to the sighting of a route onto the North Col, between Everest and Changtse. Mallory was convinced the northern side was the key to the summit as Tibet, India and the south were politically out of bounds at the time. At last they reached this Col, at 7000m (22,970ft), from where they could look up the snow ridge which meets the Northeast Ridge at 8350m (27,400ft). Fierce winds forced them to retreat, but Mallory was sure the route would be possible in one of the rare periods of calm.

Six months later he was back, as a member of the 1922 expedition. It started off very well, with the group making steady progress up the unknown slopes. Sadly, it ended unpropitiously, with seven Sherpas killed on the lower ridge. They retreated with a height of 8300m (27,232ft) to their credit. Mallory said: 'I will be back!'

Top left Sherpa Tenzing Norgay on Everest. According to Edmund Hillary, they arrived at the top together.
Centre left Martin Boysen, Doug Scott and Ronnie Richards preparing a meal at Camp IV, Mount Everest.
Bottom left A paralyzed Sherpa being rescued from a crevasse in an icefall in extreme conditions on Everest.
Opposite The dangerous broken ground of the giant Khumbu Icefall can be seen in Everest's Western Cwm.

In 1924 he was, as lead climber on the expedition led by Colonel Edward Norton. Mallory was a refined and intelligent man with a passion for books and poetry. He spent a lot of time with Dr Howard Somervell, the two gaining renown for reading Shakespeare to each other in their tent.

Mallory eventually paired himself with Andrew Irvine – an Oxford student, a strong climber, and an expert on the new oxygen systems. Somervell and Norton had already pushed a route across the vast North Face to the huge couloir (the Norton Couloir) – a new record height of 8580m (28,150ft). Mallory, however, decided to eschew this route, and he and Irvine moved straight up the ridge, in perfect weather. Noel Odell (UK), at Camp V, saw the pair at just on 13:00, going strongly immediately above the great Rock Step. That was the last anyone ever saw of them, and the oft-debated question remains whether the pair in reality deserves the title of the 'First Everest Summitteers' or not.

A further four expeditions to the North Ridge preceded World War II, all unsuccessful because of heavy and unseasonable snowfalls. Yet another unsuccessful attempt was the 'unofficial' one of

the eccentric Maurice Wilson, who in 1933 flew (solo) to India in his tiny Gypsy Moth named *Ever-Wrest*. He aimed to crash-land his plane on the slopes, and then 'walk up the peak'. He was (understandably) refused permission to fly there, so instead hired Sherpas and walked in. He then

climbed the North Ridge route, but disappeared near the North Col, his Sherpas eventually having deserted 'the mad man' in despair. His remains regularly surface from the snow on the slopes below the Col, a grim reminder to climbers of their own mortality and of another's somewhat insane determination.

World War II put paid to all activity on the peak, and then the Dalai Lama's horoscope warned him against foreigners, which effectively closed Tibet to climbers. Nepal, too, was in political turmoil, but by 1951 things had improved sufficiently to allow a reconnaissance expedition, wanting to examine the great Western Cwm of Mallory's notes, to walk in to Everest. The group consisted of four British climbers, with Eric Shipton as leader (a quick-tempered but hardy climber, who had been on all four 1930s attempts), Bill Murray, Tom Bourdillon, Mike Ward, and two New Zealand additions, Earle Riddiford and Edmund Hillary. Their survey managed to determine the route in along the Khumbu Glacier and Icefall as far as the Western Cwm, but there

Top left Porters at the foot of the North Col, 1922.

Top right Morshead, Mallory, Somervell and Norton during the 1922 expedition, with clothing typical of the period.

Left George Mallory and Edward Norton at 8300m (27,232ft) on Northeast Ridge, the highest point reached in 1922.

a giant crevasse stopped them. They were none-theless convinced that the way lay there.

An entertaining sequel to this expedition comprised the 'Yeti track' photographs provided by Shipton, a man known for a sense of mischief, and one who would never admit whether they constituted a hoax or were real. The elusive Yeti – the 'half-human, half-animal' creature is firmly embedded in local folklore – remains a mystery on Everest, with locals providing scraps of in-formation, but no expedition has yet provided photographic or other evidence of its existence. Perhaps a climber may yet come face to face with this mythical beast!

Quick to cash in on the southern route were the Swiss, who gained permission for a 1952 attempt. They took five days to find a route through the dangerous Khumbu Icefall, which they nicknamed the 'suicide passage', and then over the crevasse. The route then traversed the Lhotse Glacier, and eventually swept back towards the South Col.

Raymond Lambert, with Tenzing Norgay, and René Aubert along with Léon Flory set out from the Col on 27 May: destination – the summit ridge, and thence the summit. At 8380m (27,500ft) they decided to bivouac, but with only one small tent and little food, only Lambert and Tenzing remained for a summit bid. They spent a freezing night, with-out sleeping bags or stove, hugging and slapping each other to keep warm. The next day the already

Top right Great controversy surrounded this pic-ture of the scalp of a Yeti displayed by Kancha Sherpa at Pangboche Monastery, Khumbu.

Above The 1922 expedition finding its way through ice towers on the Upper Rongbuk Glacier.

exhausted pair set off for the South Summit, but turned back at the rock band just below it. In the words of Lambert: 'The decision was taken with-out words. One long look, and then the descent. Was it an altitude record? No, failure. That is what we thought. But did we think? Our bodies were made of lead, almost without spirit. Our muscles no longer obeyed our orders. Pick up your left foot and put it in front; now the other. Our tracks up had almost vanished. We stopped as often as on the ascent. We went on, kept in motion only by the will to resist the lethargy that was invading us.'

The pair collapsed just before reaching the tents on the South Col, and their partners dragged them into safety. The valiant Swiss attempt was over.

SUCCESS AT LAST

The British knew 1953 *had* to be the successful attempt on 'their' mountain. Much as the French were associated with Annapurna, the Germans with Nanga Parbat and the Italians with K2, so Everest had been primarily a British affair. The French had booked for 1954, and England's national honour was at stake.

A strong team was assembled, including Tenzing Norgay, Edmund Hillary, Tom Bourdillon, George Lowe, Alf Gregory and Charles Evans, under the leadership of Colonel John Hunt. The team moved swiftly but cautiously over now-familiar territory, until Bourdillon and Evans reached the South Summit, at 8762m (28,750ft), only 100m (300ft)

below the true summit. Weary and frustrated, they had no choice but to turn back from the wildly corniced ridge, knowing that victory was in sight for some other summit pair. As a final gesture, they left their half-full oxygen bottles on the ridge.

Two days later, Hillary and Tenzing were ready for a second bid at the high camp (8500m; 27,900ft) established by Lowe, Gregory and a Sherpa, Ang Nyima. Hillary had an impressive record of climbs in his native New Zealand and elsewhere, and Tenzing had a great deal of Everest experience; the pair made a formidable team.

At 04:00 on 29 May they prepared to leave their precarious mountain womb. It took over an hour to thaw Hillary's boots over a candle. They set off up the ridge, picking up the stashed oxygen on the way. The snow was firm, so they could traverse along the 'great contorted cornices which stuck out like twisted fingers over the 3050m (10,000ft) drop of the Kangshung Face. I realized that our margin of safety at this altitude was not great, and that we must take every precaution'. (Hillary, from *Everest* –

Above Hillary outside the hospital he founded at Kunde. He and his wife have done much to uplift the health and education of the Sherpas.

Left Preparing for their successful attempt — Hillary is checking the flow rate of the capricious oxygen set on Tenzing's back.

the best writing and pictures from 70 years of endeavour). After an hour they reached a seemingly impenetrable 12m (40ft) rock barrier. Hillary told himself: 'Ed, my boy, this is Everest.' Digging into his reserves, he wriggled up a crack and surmounted the barrier – now aptly named the Hillary Step.

The ridge forced them to cut steps, an exhausting job at over 8800m (28,870ft). 'I wondered rather dully just how long we could keep it up. Our original zest had now quite gone, and it was turning more into a grim struggle. I then realized that the ridge ahead, instead of still monotonously rising, now dropped sharply away, and far below I could see the North Col and the Rongbuk Glacier. I looked upwards to see a narrow snow ridge running up to a snowy summit. A few more whacks of the ice axe in the firm snow and we stood on top. It was 11.30 am. The ridge had taken us two and a half hours, but it seemed like a lifetime.' (Ibid.)

Top As dawn breaks, the peak of Lhotse (centre) seems to overshadow Everest, with Everest's Kangshung Face emerging from the shadows.

Right Climbers on the summit, Norwegian Everest Expedition, 1985. Everest dwarfs its surrounding peaks, most of which exceed 7000m (23,000ft).

The highest summit had been climbed, and the world rejoiced in the victors' triumph and safe return. Exhausted, Hillary, Tenzing and the rest returned home, thankful that their climb had not exacted the dreadful toll which the ascent of many of the other 8000m peaks had taken on their climbers. The way up Everest had been found, now the giant peak awaited new routes, new ventures.

Many expeditions followed. The first new route was the Chinese completion of the Northeast Ridge in 1960. Americans William Unsoeld and Thomas Hornbein climbed the huge West Ridge in 1963, traversed off into a narrow couloir (now called the Hornbein Couloir) and descended via South Col, with a forced bivouac at 8500m (27,890ft) in which frostbite cost Unsoeld nine of his toes.

THE SOUTHWEST FACE

The next new route came only in 1975, when the first two British climbers summitted via the imposing Southwest Face. This is still regarded as one of the most spectacular and demanding routes on Everest.

The Nepalese Southwest Face above the Khumbu Icefall is a real challenge. Steep and unforgiving, it offers an elegant direct line to the summit. The *diretissima* (*see* page 159) was eventually not to be; the awesome rock band in the upper quarter of the face defeated all attempts to forge directly upwards. The eventual route was forced inevitably towards the South Ridge and South Summit. Five expeditions (the Japanese in 1969, 1970 and 1973; the International expedition of 1971; and Bonington's earlier attempt in 1972) attempted this face before success was achieved by the British group led by Chris Bonington in 1975. All stumbled at the formidable 300m (1000ft) yellow rock band beginning around the 8200m (27,000ft) line: not only does the band enforce impossibly difficult rock climbing for the altitude; this crumbling formation also pelts rocks down on all lower camps, vastly increasing the danger.

The decision was made to attempt the face siege-style, since a fast, light, alpine-style ascent over the complex territory may not have worked. Bonington used his organizational abilities to secure sponsorship, arrange equipment and other

planning, and select the team of 10 climbers, all highly regarded in climbing circles. (This was a large team by British standards; the Japanese in comparison had 36 climbers in 1970.) The group was supported by nine climbers (base-camp managers, communications personnel and doctors), a five-person BBC film crew and 75 Sherpas. They

Opposite A climber using oxygen high on Everest's North Ridge, with Rongbuk Glacier below.

had state-of-the-art equipment and no expense was spared. By 31 August, all were in Advance Base Camp at 6610m (21,700ft), high up in the Western Cwm, among the walls of Lhotse, Nuptse and Everest. Over three tons of supplies had to be moved up from base camp to here.

Camp V was set up at 7620m (25,000ft) by 16 September. The next objective was the notorious Rock Band. Paul (Tut) Braithwaite and Nick Estcourt eventually found and completed a route, and the way upward lay open. A single 'summit box' – an aluminium-framed box tent – was sited at 8320m (27,300ft) on a tiny snow terrace above the rock band. The summit bids were launched from here. The first was made by Doug Scott and Dougal Haston, and the angled rock terraces led them up to a gully just under the South Summit and onto the summit ridge. The Hillary Step, snow-covered in the post-monsoon season, went easily by, and then it was a case of negotiating the ridge. Dougal wrote: 'We were sampling a unique moment in our lives. On the north and east sides there was a sense of wildness and remoteness, almost untouchability.' The pair summitted at 18:00, and were forced to spend a hungry night in a small snow cave they dug on the South Summit.

Below A Sherpa team in the Western Cwm below Nuptse's North Face en route to Camp II.

Above A climber on the 1996 South African Everest Expedition using a ladder on the icefall.

Below The steep, dangerous cliffs of the Northeast Ridge of Everest, as seen from the south.

THE PHYSIOLOGY OF HIGH-ALTITUDE CLIMBING

One might wonder why the 8000m (26,000ft) peaks are so hard to climb. For many years it was believed that no-one could live at such high altitudes and, even when the first ascent of Everest took place in 1953, there was doubt as to whether anyone could survive on the summit for any length of time, with or without supplementary oxygen. Many ascents of the 8000m peaks have since taken place without oxygen, and there has been no noticeable damage to the climbers' brains, nor has it affected their other functions, so this question has now been resolved. Many other questions remain, however, unanswered, particularly those dealing with the mechanisms behind the body's deterioration at high altitude. It is difficult to expound adequately the problems of working at altitude, and how these are exacerbated by cold, high winds, lack of adequate sleep and nutrition, and general physical exhaustion.

The human body is in many ways no more than a biological machine. Any sophisticated machine needs two main driving factors: energy and control.

ENERGY

The body gets the energy it needs from the burning, or oxidation, of foodstuffs, which are either found stored in the body tissue or obtained from digestion. In order to oxidize the food stored in the body cells, it is metabolized aerobically (via a metabolic pathway which needs oxygen) or anaerobically (without immediate use of oxygen). All chemical reactions progress best at an optimum temperature; for most of the metabolic enzymes this is close to 37°C

(98.6°F), or normal body temperature. From these facts arise the three main problems of altitude:

1. The lack of oxygen — As one gains height, so the air pressure drops, and thus also the amount of available oxygen. Not only is there less oxygen, but there is also less pressure to force what oxygen there is across the lung tissue 'barriers' into the blood, and in addition the oxygen-transporting blood haemoglobin is less ready to absorb the oxygen molecules. The pressure on top of Everest is less than a third of the pressure at sea level, therefore the body attempts to compensate by doing more work anaerobically. The disadvantage of this is that it is a less efficient way to 'burn' foods, and it also builds up wastes such as lactic acid in muscle tissue, leading to stiffness and soreness. These wastes in turn can only be removed in the presence of oxygen, leading to an escalating

DOUGAL HASTON CLIMBING THE EVEREST SOUTHWEST FACE ON OXYGEN, 1975 EXPEDITION.

SUNSET OVER MOUNT EVEREST (LEFT), LHOTSE (CENTRE) AND NUPTSE (RIGHT).

and debilitating 'oxygen debt' in the body of any climber who remains for long periods at altitude.

2. Food – Climbers are limited in what they can carry up steep slopes, the more so at altitude, where muscles function inefficiently. This weakness is aggravated by the nausea often experienced at heights, leading to a low food intake. Food cannot be cooked properly, as water boils at very low temperatures (as low as 30°C; 86°F). Snow (often the only source of water) takes a lot of crucial fuel to melt, and a lot of snow melts down to very little water. Thus dehydration is also common, compounded by the cold, dry air, leading to even lower food absorption than usual.

3. Cold – This has multiple effects, not least being that it decreases metabolism, inhibits oxygen transfer and increases the chance of injuries. It also plays the major role in frostbite and hypothermia. The psychological effects should also not be underestimated.

A CLIMBER MELTS SNOW IN THE MOUNTAINS OF PERU. REPLACING LOST WATER IS ESSENTIAL AT ALTITUDE.

CONTROL

Don Whillans, renowned British climber, when asked how to train for altitude, reputedly said: 'Go out to a pub and get motherlessly drunk every night – because this is what it feels like when you're up there!' His humorous comment is close to the truth; headaches, lack of co-ordination, poor reflexes and worse judgement – these are the hallmarks of altitude. Even the morning hangover is there! Sleep is not easy; the lack of air, the cold, wind noise, and general tiredness and

feeling of malaise often lead to sleepless nights, which compound the problem the next night, ad infinitum. High-altitude climbers often take hours to do simple things like putting on boots or lighting a stove. The brain, reliant on a good oxygen supply for coherent thought, slows down. Simple climbing becomes desperately difficult; reactions and all decisions are suspect.

Watching climbers at high altitude is rather like watching an old-fashioned movie: it seems to happen in slow motion – a step, then a long pause, then another jerky step. There is truly no way that these poor souls can move any faster – their minds and bodies, no matter how fit, simply won't let them.

Acclimatization, achieved by gaining altitude very slowly, or spending long periods of time at increasingly higher altitudes, does help, but to a limited extent. The body deteriorates above 5000m (16,000ft), and the longer one stays at this altitude, the worse it will be. Staying longer than a few days will cause weight loss and deterioration of mental function – fortunately these symptoms are usually only temporary!

Above Guides and Sherpas help a client after an unsuccessful summit bid.

Above Guide Rob Hall tells his client to return – it is too late in the day to continue to the summit.

Above Israeli climber Doran Erel, pictured here on the Hillary Step during a guided trip.

Another group headed for the summit – Per Temba (the head Sherpa) with Peter Boardman, Martin Boysen and Mick Burke. Boysen turned back with a faulty oxygen cylinder, but the rest kept going. Boardman and Per Temba summitted at 13:00 and, on their way back, saw Burke plodding upwards. They agreed to wait at the South Summit, but had to leave to avoid an enforced bivouac in a vicious storm. Eventually the group had to accept that Mick Burke had died. They abandoned the mountain just as massive avalanches started to sweep down the slopes.

LIGHT AND FAST

In 1983 three Americans – Robert Anderson, Ed Webster and Paul Teare – along with Briton Stephen Venables attempted the Kangshung Face. This 3000m (10,000ft) face, constantly swept by avalanches, was finally climbed by a US expedition on the third attempt. The first unsuccessful try, in 1981, included Edmund Hillary and Kurt Diemberger; the 1983 attempt included the controversial use of a rocket launcher and an aerial cableway to haul loads over the first 1000m-high (3500ft) rock and ice buttress.

The 1983 quartet climbed without porters or oxygen. Using a line parallel with the existing American route, they completed the difficult climb of the lower face and reached the South Col on 10 May. The team was exhausted, but Venables reached the top, solo, at 15:50 – very late for safety on the way down. Venables later wrote evocatively of the hallucinations brought on by altitude and exhaustion, including an 'invisible companion' – an old man who moved with him, occasionally speaking and offering advice. At 21:00, at 8500m (27,900ft) Venables, lost, writes: 'The old man suggested that we stop here for the night, and wait for daylight to re-orientate ourselves. We traversed back out onto the snow, and dug a horizontal ledge where we could lie down properly.' He knew that he was dehydrated and that frostbite was likely. The next morning he stumbled and glissaded down to meet his companions on the South Col. His frostbite fears were to prove true – he lost three toes. Still, he paid a small price compared to others, such as Unsoeld and Hornbein who lost virtually all their toes after their 8500m (27,900ft) bivouac; two British soldiers, Bronco Lane (all fingers and toes) and Brummie Stokes (all toes); and Hannelore Schmatz, whose frozen body periodically reappeared on the Southeast Ridge for some years before it was released by an avalanche.

Left In this view of the Summit Pyramid, the Great Couloir, first ascended by two Australians in 1984, dominates the North Face.

One of the boldest climbs was that of Reinhold Messner, whose solo of the new 'North Col to Norton Couloir route' without oxygen in August 1980 spurred on a new attitude to high-altitude peaks.

THE MODERN EVEREST

Everest today has many climbers in any one season. The summit total, just over 480 in the 39 years up to 1992, has almost doubled in the last five years to over 840. The mountains are seen as a source of revenue by Nepalese and Tibetan authorities, and the number of permits issued per year has escalated. 'Guided' trips, if one can afford the US$65,000-odd per person, have been the subject of huge controversy, particularly after the disastrous deaths of 10 climbers in 1996. Two professional guides (Rob Hall and Scott Fisher) and their parties were stranded in a storm high on Everest, largely as a result of overcrowding of the ropes on the Hillary Step, poor planning, and plain bad luck. Both guides, an assistant guide and two clients died, raising many questions about the advisability of guiding on mountains such as Everest. However, it is worth remembering the early Alpine years, when guides and climbers pushed the limits together on the great mountain faces of Europe. The essence of climbing has always been the individual's freedom of choice as to how far to go.

An interesting feat was that of Goran Kropp, a Swede who cycled to Nepal from Stockholm, carried in all his food and equipment, and climbed the standard route, solo, in May 1996. The 'Highest Peak in the World' still holds many challenges for extreme climbers, including new routes and variations on some of the more technical faces.

Finally, the words of Sir Edmund Hillary: 'I am thankful that I climbed Everest in the days of innocence, when everything was new and a constant challenge. I feel sorry for today's climbers trying to find something new and interesting to do on the mountain, something that will get both the public's attention and the respect of their peers. Recent ascents include some great and heroic efforts – I am sure there will be more in the future.'

Right A climber above the Hillary Step, Southeast Ridge. This deceptively easy-looking step becomes a major challenge at this extreme altitude.

Annapurna

First of the 8000s to Succumb

The ascent of Annapurna created fresh interest in high-altitude mountaineering, being the first peak over the 'magic' 8000m (26,000ft) to be climbed. It was also the first major peak to be conquered on the first attempt, without prior reconnaissance. When the French team, led by Maurice Herzog, entered the region, they had no information on the peak; even their knowledge of its whereabouts was sketchy. They entered Nepal on 5 April 1950, and spent two weeks travelling the 140km (90 miles) to Tukucha, the site of their base camp. They planned to 'recce' Dhaulagiri (8167m; 26,796ft) and Annapurna, both of which had been photographed from a distance by the 1949 Swiss aerial survey.

After three weeks of exploration, the group concluded that Dhaulagiri was 'impossible', and they turned their attention to the elusive Annapurna. In mid-May the doctor, Jacques Oudot, along with Marcel Schatz and Jean Couzy, found a route above the impassable gorges of the Miristi Khola River which gave access to the foot of the glacier below the Northwest Spur of Annapurna. There was less than a month to the probable start of the monsoon, so they set up camp at 4600m (15,000ft) at the glacier foot. Advance Base was soon moved up to a safer spot at 5090m (16,700ft).

Lionel Terray and Louis Lachenal, who had together done the second ascent of the Eiger North Face, ploughed through snow, ice and rock (up to Grade V – a truly hard grade at this altitude) to

ANNAPURNA 8091m

Sickle Ice Cliff

—— *North Face (Herzog) 1950*

reach 4570m (15,584ft) on the Northwest Spur by 21 May. This route was then abandoned as being too difficult, in particular for the Sherpas, and they decided to try the North Glacier. A route was found along the flank of the great icefall; thereafter three camps, the highest at 6888m (22,600ft), were set up on the glacier. To reach Camp III involved the 'hell run' – a 200m (700ft) steep ice slope with constant danger of avalanches.

After pushing the route to Camp IV, Terray and Gaston Rébuffat were exhausted, as were Couzy and Schatz. Herzog and Lachenal, more rested, pushed on to establish Camp IVA and a precarious Camp V at 7450m (24,443ft). Their tent was anchored to one piton on a platform chopped into the slope above the immense Sickle.

The rest of the climbers moved laboriously up to Camp IVA to support the summit bid, bringing supplies that proved vital for their eventual retreat.

After a restless night, worried that their tiny tent would be swept by sliding snow into the abyss below, Lachenal and Herzog set off into a storm. Their equipment was minimal, to save weight. They left even their rope behind, and chose lighter boots – this they would later regret. They climbed up the huge tilted Northeast Face, concerned about frostbite, their feet already numb. Lachenal asked what Herzog would do if he turned back; the latter said he would continue alone, but that Lachenal was free to choose. Lachenal kept going.

Opposite Annapurna South Face (first ascent 1970) seen from the convoluted ridge between camps IV and V.

Top right A radio aerial helps Annapurna Base Camp to maintain communication with those on the mountain.

Bottom right Flying spindrift reflects the typical strong winds encountered on all high Himalayan peaks.

Herzog wrote: 'Nothing could stop us from getting to the top. The psychological atmosphere changed with these few words, and we went forward now as brothers. Stopping at every step, leaning on our axes, trying to recover our breath and to calm our hearts, which were thumping as though they would burst, we dragged ourselves up. A fierce and savage wind tore at us. Could we possibly be there? Yes! We were on top of Annapurna.'

The descent was a nightmare. Herzog lost his gloves, the pair became separated and Lachenal fell down a steep slope, losing his hat, gloves, ice axe and a crampon, and ending up well below Camp V. Luckily Terray and Rébuffat had, at great risk, come up to Camp V with another tent, and could help the now badly frostbitten pair back to the shelter of a tent. The weather was horrendous. Tired, dazed and terrified of frostbite, Lachenal fought with his rescuers in a bid to go down to Oudot, their doctor – which would have been suicidal. Rébuffat and Terray persuaded him to stay; they massaged the feet and hands of the summit pair throughout the night, made hot drinks and tried to keep their spirits up. Next morning they started descending, often losing their way in the whiteout trying to locate the tortuous route to Camp IV. That night, with only one sleeping bag among the four of them, they bivouacked in a crevasse that gave them shelter from the incessant wind.

Above Climbers at Annapurna Base Camp keenly watching the moves of a team's summit bid.

Next day Terray and Rébuffat were snow blind, having forgotten about the intensity of UV light through cloud and gone without snow-goggles the day before. The crippled pair of Herzog and Lachenal had to guide their physically more able helpers. This sad sight greeted the eyes of Schatz, who had come up from Camp IVA to look for them.

Right Evening light illuminates Machapuchare, which lies in the centre of the Annapurna Himal.

The two blind and two crippled Frenchmen were escorted by their two compatriots and six Sherpas down steep, avalanche-prone slopes in a constant blizzard. At Camp II, Oudot performed excruciatingly painful injections into their arteries and nerve ganglia in an attempt to arrest the frostbite by increasing the circulation. This was followed up during the return journey by repeated sad but unavoidable amputations, performed with no anaesthetic under deplorable conditions. In the end, despite the best care possible, Lachenal lost all his toes, and Herzog most of his fingers and all his toes.

The Sherpas carried the pair in wicker baskets down to base camp, and then rushed along difficult, slippery tracks to the first road transport in a race to beat the full force of the monsoon. At times the group feared for the safety of the invalids as porters teetered along ledges above drops of hundreds of feet, or balanced on bridges made of tree

trunks, spanning raging torrents. The team press-ganged villagers into acting as unwilling (albeit well-paid) porters, to escape from the Himalayas before the arrival of the monsoon closed off all the river crossings. Despite the haste, it took them a full month to reach the railhead in Nautanwa.

Left Chris Bonington on the ice ridge between camps IV and V, South Face, first ascent 1970.

Below Porters arriving at base camp, with Dhaulagiri across the valley. Even at this early point, a slip could spell disaster.

'Annapurna, to which we had gone empty-handed, was a treasure on which we should live the rest of our days. With this realization we turn the page, a new life begins. There are other Annapurnas in the lives of men.' (Maurice Herzog, *Annapurna – Conquest of the First 8000m Peak*)

Herzog then went on to become the Minister of Sport for France. Annapurna was left well alone for a long time; there was an unsuccessful German expedition in 1969, but the conquest remained unrepeated until the 1970 British Army expedition to the North Face, and the South Face expedition.

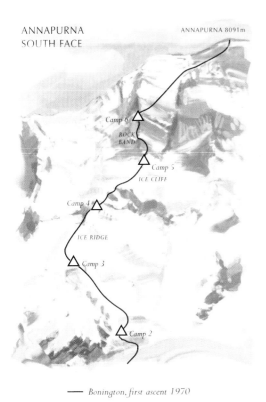

ANNAPURNA
SOUTH FACE

ANNAPURNA 8091m

Camp 6
ROCK
BAND

Camp 5
ICE CLIFF

Camp 4

ICE RIDGE

Camp 3

Camp 2

—— Bonington, first ascent 1970

Right According to Bonington, the South Face was like four Alpine faces piled on top of one another.

Below Dougal Haston, high up on the South Face during the first ascent in 1970.

ANNAPURNA'S SOUTH FACE

The year 1970 was rather unusual in that two different British expeditions were tackling the very same peak – the Army was approaching from the north, and a strong expedition under the leadership of Chris Bonington from the un-explored south. The latter group had managed to assemble the cream of British climbers (Martin Boysen, Nick Estcourt, Dougal Haston, Don Whillans, Ian Clough and Mick Burke) as well as Tom Frost from the USA; the team was also supplemented by Mike Thompson (liaison), Dr Dave Lambert, and Kelvin Kent, from the Gurkha signals corps. The group also had a four-man television crew with them.

The expedition was very well organized, al-though the climbers in effect had great freedom in deciding their roles and movements. With this combination, they made rapid progress on the huge wall of Annapurna South; after only four days, Camp II was already established at 5333m

(17,500ft) on the central rib, or pillar. Only then did the onslaught begin in earnest, with the route up to Camp VI, at 7315m (24,000ft), con-taining a number of Grade 5+ rock pitches. Nothing had ever been done at this altitude that compared even remotely with the difficulties needing to be overcome here.

On 27 May, Don Whillans and Dougal Haston pushed through the remaining 1500m (5000ft) without oxygen, reaching the summit in heavy cloud and strong winds – a phenomenal feat. What distinguished the attempt even more was that, notwithstanding the support of the large group, a good deal of the ascent was actually made alpine-style – small, lightweight parties, carrying all their own gear and equipment from camp to camp. It gave rise to a whole new era in Himalayan mountaineering.

Sadly Ian Clough was killed on 30 May, crushed by a falling sérac (see page 159) between camps I and II – a tragic end to a successful ascent.

The Killer Mountain

The undistinguished name of K2 gives no indication of the majestic and difficult nature of the peak. Reinhold Messner (*see* page 11), the first climber to ascend all 14 of the 8000m (26,000ft) summits (*see* page 158), gave it the doubtful accolade of being 'more difficult than any other 8000m peak'. The facts undoubtedly bear this out – in the years since its first ascent, K2 has had the lowest success rate and highest death rate of them all.

K2 has a fascinating history, perhaps even more so than Everest. The name K2 arose when, in 1856, Captain T G Montgomerie of the British Survey of India saw this peak and the surrounding ones from a distance of 180km (120 miles). He named the peaks according to their apparent height: K1 (K for Karakoram), K2 and so on. (Masherbrum was accorded the name K1, as it seemed to be higher than Chogori, or K2.)

The first European to get near K2 was Henry Godwin-Austen (UK), who in 1861 tried to find a path through the New Mustagh Pass to create the easiest route between India, China and Russia (of critical military importance). He failed to get further than the Baltoro Glacier.

In 1887 Francis Younghusband (UK) found a guide, Wali, who promised to take him over the fabled Old Mustagh Pass. They eventually located the 5800m (19,000ft) gap, and made an epic descent down the steep, icy northern slopes. The

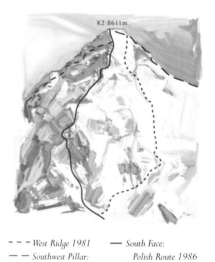

- - - *West Ridge 1981* —— *South Face:*
— — *Southwest Pillar:*   *Polish Route 1986*
    'Magic Line' 1986 ··· *Abruzzi Ridge 1954*

guide was nearly lynched by his fellow villagers for betraying the whereabouts of the pass, perhaps with good reason – four years later the village was invaded via the same gap.

William Martin Conway, an art professor, and Charles Bruce, both British, led an expedition to K2 in 1892; it failed, because of friction between Oscar Eckenstein, an Austrian climber, and Matthias Zurbriggen, a Swiss guide. The two refused to climb together, Eckenstein because of Zurbriggen's 'slow, old-fashioned ways', and Zurbriggen because Eckenstein was 'a tinkerer and an amateur'. Eckenstein, an engineer, is credited with inventing strap-on, 10-point, full-boot crampons, as well as revolutionary ice-axe heads.

The positive side of Conway's expedition was that he developed excellent maps, and this helped to change the old-fashioned attitude towards climbing, paving the way for patronage in later expeditions.

In 1902 an unusual team made its argumentative way to K2 under the leadership of Eckenstein, now living in England. With him were, among others, Jules Guillarmod, a Swiss doctor; Victor Wesseley, a Viennese judge; Guy Knowles, a British engineer who financed the expedition; and the eccentric British 'black magician', Aleister Crowley.

From Askole the party thought that 'they could climb the peak in three or four days'. Many early expeditions misjudged the size of these peaks –

Top left A climber is dwarfed by the vastness of the face – the scale of the Karakoram peaks is huge.
Bottom left Descent from Uli Biaho, Baltoro Glacier – descents can be even more hazardous than ascents.
Opposite A view of K2 from Godwin-Austen Glacier. The unforgiving Abruzzi Ridge leads up on the right.

THE KARAKORAM

The Karakoram lies at the northern extremity of the Himalayas, between India and the endless steppes of Tibet. The entire region is rich in climbing sites, but the Baltoro region, centred on the bowl containing the Baltoro Glacier, has the finest selection of immense, challenging summits. These include K2 (8611m; 28,253ft), Broad Peak (8047m; 26,402ft), Gasherbrum IV (7980m; 26,182ft), III (7925m; 26,001ft), II (8035m; 26,363ft) and I (Hidden Peak – 8068m; 26,471ft), as well as Chogolisa (7645m; 25,083ft), the Mustagh Tower (7263m; 23,830ft) and, a little off to one side, Nanga Parbat (8125m; 26,658ft) and the Trango Towers (6250m; 20,500ft).

ABOVE AND RIGHT THE COMPLEX SYSTEM OF GLACIERS, RIDGES AND HIGH PEAKS IN THE KARAKORAM RANGE OFFERS SOME OF THE MOST CHALLENGING HIGH-ALTITUDE CLIMBING IN THE WORLD.

Sir Francis Younghusband recorded: 'The glaciers and valleys were so well adjusted in their proportions to the surrounding mountains that it was hard to realize the true size of any object.'

It took the group 10 days of hard travel just to reach the end of the Baltoro Glacier. The fights which had dogged the expedition began afresh as Crowley spotted a line on the 2000m-long (6562ft) Southeast (Abruzzi) Ridge, with its 45-degree line to the shoulder. But Guy Knowles favoured the Northeast Ridge, and an argument simmered throughout the climb. When, at 6000m (19,686ft), Knowles proposed retreat on 'his' line, Crowley in his frustration, semi-delirious with malaria, threatened him with a large revolver. The pair struggled on the brink of a precipice, until Knowles managed to disarm Crowley. (Knowles' companions later warned him, not entirely in jest, to beware lest Crowley turn him into a horned toad!)

THE ABRUZZI RIDGE

In 1909 an Italian party made a more disciplined approach. The huge expedition – 6000kg (13,230 lb) of luggage, 500 porters, and 11 climbers led by Amedeo di Savoia – the Duke of Abruzzi and nephew of King Victor Emmanuel I – wound its way to the base of the Southeast Ridge. They too

only reached just over 6000m (19,686ft) before being forced to abandon the attempt, disheartened despite the fact that the Abruzzi Ridge was the steepest ever attempted in the Himalayas at that time. Abruzzi commented: 'One could not hope to complete so long and formidable a climb when, from the start, one is faced with such overwhelming difficulties. K2 will surely never be climbed!' This comment, along with amazing photographs by the incomparable photographer Vittorio Sella, did much to glamorize the peak.

The extreme difficulty of K2 discouraged further attempts until 1938, when Dr Charles Houston, fresh from the first ascent of Nandi Devi, led a five-person American group accompanied by six experienced Sherpas. They attempted the Northwest Ridge, but gave up at a little over 6300m (20,670ft). They then moved onto the Abruzzi Ridge, and established their Camp V at 6550m (21,490ft). One of the group, William (Bill) House, led a desperate chimney crack, now known as House's Chimney and acknowledged as the key to the mountain, to open the route to Camp VI and then on to Camp VII at 7525m (24,689ft).

Then a minor tragedy arose from a tiny oversight. The team established Houston and Paul Petzoldt in Camp VII, ready for a summit bid, and

left them there overnight – lonely figures, perched higher than any other human. To their horror, the pair discovered that they had no matches, which meant no flame, therefore no warm fluids or cooked food. The next day they nonetheless pushed on as far as the base of the summit pyramid, but were compelled to retreat, cold and disappointed, having been within a few hundred metres of their goal.

Houston's comment, in conflict with Abruzzi's, was: 'With a bit of luck, our successors will reach the summit.' What brought about such a change in outlook? Was it the advances of equipment, or the alteration of climbing style? Perhaps the successes on other 'impossible' peaks such as Nandi Devi brought about the optimism of Houston. He was to be proven right, but not until 1954. Long before then came the 1939 disaster.

Dudley Wolfe, an American millionaire, teamed up with a German (newly American) adventurer, Fritz Wiessner, determined to climb K2. Wiessner had recently stunned American climbers by making the first ascent of Devil's Tower, an imposing rock spire in Wyoming. Wiessner warned Wolfe that he lacked experience. Three other young climbers, also not very experienced at altitude, were invited along.

Things started well, with good weather allowing a series of camps to be established leading up the Abruzzi Ridge to Camp VII. Then the team started to fall apart, with frostbite, pulmonary oedema and exhaustion claiming victim after victim. Wolfe, Wiessner and Sherpa Pasang Lama managed to

Opposite top Kurt Diemberger on the Abruzzi Ridge during the tragic 1986 season.

Opposite bottom Gary Ball is pictured here using fixed ropes on the Abruzzi Ridge.

Above Climbers brave windy conditions on Broad Peak with K2 looming in the background.

settle in at Camp VII with sufficient supplies to attempt the peak or wait for a break in the weather.

Disaster then intervened. Jack Durrance, one of the young climbers, succumbed to altitude sickness at Camp VI and decided to go down to Camp II. It snowed continuously for two days, then intermittently for four. Durrance gave the fateful order for Camps I to IV to be cleared, not imagining that the top pair would still be climbing. Wolfe and Wiessner meanwhile did push on, setting up Camp VIII and even Camp IX, at 7940m (26,051ft).

Two Sherpas were sent up to Camp VII to help them down and, finding no signs of life, assumed the worst and cleared all camps down to base camp.

By 18:00 Wiessner, oblivious to this, had climbed to 8382m (27,501ft), just short of the summit

ridge. His companion, Sherpa Pasang Lama, now refused to go any further. He was scared of the 'evil spirits that gathered on the mountain at night'. The disgruntled Wiessner was forced to return to Camp IX, where Wolfe waited. On the way, the pair lost their crampons off the back of a pack.

The next day they tried again, but got no higher. On return to Camp IX, they found that the supplies hadn't arrived, and, having no food or matches, decided to leave their equipment in Camp VIII and descend to Camp VII to find out what was wrong. They found to their horror that the ridge had been cleared. Wolfe, exhausted, was left at the site of Camp VII, and the others managed to descend to base camp. A furious scene ensued. The Sherpas heroically attempted to reach Wolfe, and finally

did so two days later, to find him totally helpless. They tried to feed him, but he was too ill to eat. They climbed down to the re-established Camp VI to report this, and went back up the next day. A storm forced the rest of the group to leave the mountain, and subsequently no one could get back up to Camp VII despite numerous efforts. Wolfe and the three Sherpas were never seen again.

There were no more attempts on K2 until 1953, when an American team returned, led by Charles Houston. They stormed the Abruzzi Ridge, and all eight climbers were soon settled at Camp VIII at 7700m (25,263ft). Then one of the worst monsoons in India's history hit. Winds were so high that tents were shredded. It was impossible to light stoves. After six days, Art Gilkey developed an embolism; it was decided to evacuate him. Knowing that the entire team could be put in danger to save this one life was no deterrent. While lowering the stretcher, a team member slipped on the ice, and one by one the 'rescuers' were dragged off their feet. The entire tangle of men and ropes hurtling down the slope was held by the axe of Pete Schoening, which prevented them from plunging over the 2500m (8202ft) drop to the Godwin-Austen Glacier below. The group first took Houston (who was injured) to Camp VII, but when they returned for Gilkey, he was missing.

Seven skeletal figures staggered into base camp after 12 days without food, to be met by their Hunza porters who had given them up for dead. The porters built a memorial cairn for Art Gilkey and the dead of the Wiessner expedition.

SUCCESS AT LAST

It was expected that the Italians or the Americans would succeed on K2. Annapurna was French; Everest, British; Nanga Parbat, German. In 1954 a strong Italian expedition arrived, determined to bring home the honours. The leader was Professor Doctor Ardito Desio. The group comprised some of the leading lights of Italian mountaineering,

Left Balti porters on Baltoro Glacier, 1995, make their heavily laden pilgrimage to base camp.

Opposite K2's height dominates, but Broad Peak impresses with its bulk. Gasherbrum is on the right.

including Walter Bonatti, Achille Compagnoni, Lino Lacedelli, Mario Puchoz, and Ubaldo Rey.

June, normally a fair-weather month, brought storms, causing delays. On 21 June, Mario Puchoz died of high-altitude pulmonary oedema – the sixth victim of K2 and another name for the Gilkey cairn. The team went on, and by 28 July had reached Camp VIII, on the top of the shoulder; on 30 July they set up Camp IX at 8060m (26,445ft). Bonatti and Mahdi (a porter) came up from Camp V, trying to get vital oxygen supplies to the rest of the team, but, exhausted after a brave push of many hours without oxygen themselves, were forced to stop just 80m (262ft) from Camp IX and cache the oxygen bottles. They then spent a desperate night out at over 8000m (26,000ft), 'clinging to life like shipwrecked sailors to a log' according to Bonatti.

The next day, Bonatti and Mahdi staggered down; Compagnoni and Lacedelli at Camp IX fetched the bottles, then pushed upwards. They ran out of oxygen on the summit ridge, but with determination toiled on without it. At 18:00 on 31 July, they finally stood on the top: first on the summit of K2.

Their descent was an epic – the pair was nearly carried away on a breaking cornice; Compagnoni tumbled into a crevasse, falling 15m (50ft) before the rope arrested his fall; they lost a glove and an ice axe; and Compagnoni slid more than 200m (656ft) to the brink of the great ice precipice before stopping by good fortune in a snow drift. However, they made it down, all in one piece, and the 'Killer Mountain' had at last been conquered.

Expedition after expedition followed the Italian one, but all were unsuccessful, until in 1977 a huge Japanese expedition with 42 climbers put six Japanese and one Pakistani climber on the summit via the Abruzzi Ridge.

With each new and successful attempt, however, one is inclined to forget the hardships and courage of early pioneers. To quote from Charles Houston on his 1938 trip: 'The 350 miles took 31 days – long, hard marches in hot, dry, spectacular country. We took a barge across the Indus – allegedly a relic from Alexander the Great – then a goatskin raft across the Braldu, then many rope-bridges, steep cliffs and sand.' Many tough, uphill days on steep slopes followed, culminating in the 130km (80-mile) trek up the Baltoro Glacier. Equipment was heavy, inefficient; food was basic. It is not the courage or the tenacity of the climbers themselves that has changed, to make routes 'easier' today.

Nanga Parbat

The Demon Mountain

Nanga Parbat is one of the most impressive and intimidating peaks in the Himalayas. It stands at the bend of the Indus River in the Punjab Himalayas. The river is at 1000m (3300ft) above sea level, thus on the southern (Rupal) side Nanga Parbat presents a 7000m (23,000ft) face, of which 4500m (14,700ft) is true technical climbing. It is the largest face in the Himalayas – and the highest rock and ice wall in the world.

NANGA PARBAT 8125m

—— *Kinshofer 1962*
– – *Messner Solo 1978*

The first attempt on Nanga Parbat was made in 1895, amazingly, in what now would be called alpine-style – a lightweight, small, fast push. It was led by Alfred Mummery, the renowned British climber, along with Lieutenant Charles Bruce (later, as General Bruce, he led the 1922 Everest expedition), John Collie, Geoffrey Hastings and two Gurkha soldiers. At first they tried the Diamir Face. Mummery got up to nearly 7000m (22,970ft) when his Gurkha companion fell ill, and they had to retreat. Heavy snowfalls made further attempts unwise, so they moved on towards the Rakhiot Rib. On a reconnaissance to the Diamir Col (6200m; 20,342ft), Mummery and the two Gurkhas vanished without trace.

In 1932 the next expedition arrived, a German-American group under the enthusiastic leadership of Willy Merkl. They were eventually forced off by poor weather. On the way home, Rand Herron slipped and fell to his death on the Cheops Pyramid, having recently boasted that 'Nanga couldn't get me'. The press reported that the Demon of Nanga had reached out for him.

Willy Merkl was back in 1934 with a strong team. Things started badly when one member, Alfred Drexel, succumbed to a lung infection soon after arriving at altitude. The group, however, soon made progress, and was within reach of the summit when a colossal storm broke. Three Germans (Wieland, Welzenbach and Merkl) and six Sherpas died, stranded in heavy snowfalls.

In 1937 Dr Carlo Wien led yet another large, experienced team. They set up Camp IV at 6300m (20,670ft), on a large, flat plateau, thought to be safe from avalanches. On the night of 14 June, with virtually the whole team and all the porters in this camp in preparation for stocking the higher camps, an avalanche swept down, obliterating the camp and killing seven climbers and nine porters. Again, fate had struck on Germany's 'destiny peak' – Nanga Parbat was gaining a fearsome reputation.

The fourth German expedition, in 1938, was, perhaps of necessity, overcautious and ended up retreating at 7000m (22,970ft) – the Moor's Head – after days of atrocious weather. Their retreat was largely also due to their discovery of the bodies of Merkl and his porter Gaylay, after which their unnerved porters refused to climb on.

In 1939 yet another German group, under Peter Aufschnaiter, tried first the Diamir side, then the Mummery Rib. They, too, retreated with no fatalities. A member of this team was Heinrich Harrer (of Eiger fame) who, with Peter Aufschnaiter, was interned in India at the outbreak of World War II.

Opposite The Rupal Face of Nanga Parbat in the Himalayas, arguably the highest wall in the world.
Top right Morning sunlight shines brightly on the precariously perched Camp II at Nanga Parbat.
Centre right A climber breaks trail across one of the extensive ice fields high on Nanga Parbat.
Bottom right Avalanches such as this one on Nanga Parbat represent a serious danger to climbers.

Their flight into Tibet and their stay with the Dalai Lama makes both interesting history and superb reading (*Seven Years in Tibet* by H Harrer).

Dr Karl Herrligkoffer, younger half-brother of Willy Merkl whom he idolized, arrived in 1953 with another all-German team, determined to climb 'their devil mountain'. For Herrligkoffer this was the start of a long relationship with Nanga Parbat. They attacked the Rakhiot Flank, and fought their way up through many storms, causing most to abandon hope of summitting. Dissension developed, and a small 'supergroup' of four climbers pushed out in front, often contrary to 'orders' from those in base camp, where Herrligkoffer constantly urged what Hermann Buhl believed was excessive caution. A small tent, ill-supplied and precariously pitched and manned by Otto Kempter and Hermann Buhl, perched at Camp V at 6895m (22,622ft). At 02:00 on 3 July, Buhl emerged from the tent. His obsession was so huge that, when Kempter himself proved unable to move out of the tent, Buhl set out alone, in the face of all Himalayan convention and wisdom, to 'try or die'.

There was an arduous task ahead of the 29-year-old climber: 1200m (3940ft) of altitude gain, and nearly 8km (5 miles) of distance along the ridge and over the Silver Saddle and Fore Peak. From heavy storms, the weather changed to breathlessly hot; Buhl later climbed in only a shirt, leaving his pack and most of his equipment behind him. He reached the summit at 19:00, after a long crawl on all fours. With no food or drink, and only a light sweater, he realized he was in trouble. Knowing that the ridge he had just climbed would be too difficult to descend, he dropped instead down the Diamir snow slopes. In error, he left his ice axe on the summit, and later lost a crampon. He decided to bivouac at nearly 8000m (26,000ft). An exceptionally warm night (only 10 degrees below freezing, not the more usual 40 below!) saved him from otherwise certain death, and he staggered down to the top camp the next day, badly frostbitten and exhausted, looking like a wizened old man. Germany had her peak at last!

Left In action on the long and formidable Southeast Spur of the Rakhiot Face in the light of dawn — the difficult top sections still lie ahead.

THE RUPAL FACE

The Rupal Face is regarded as the greatest of the big walls. It sweeps upwards, a bastion of ice, rock and snow. It was the great new challenge on Nanga Parbat after the peak had been ascended.

This face attracted Karl Herrligkoffer again and again. He led three attempts between 1963 and 1968, the party each time getting a little higher, but frustratingly unable to crack the problem.

In 1970, his fourth attempt, the party included the Messner brothers, Reinhold and Günther. Both were experienced mountaineers who had climbed since their childhood in the Tyrol. Reinhold, however, had more high-altitude experience than his younger brother, and was at the peak of condition.

The 18-strong team used experience gained on the 1964 and 1968 expeditions to push a line up the central *diretissima* of the Rupal Face, directly below the South Shoulder. They soon reached the Merkl Gully, the key to the face, and set up their high camp just below this. The five-man summit party split up, with two dropping back for rest and supplies. Eventually there were three climbers at the top camp: Reinhold, Günther and cameraman Gerhard Baur. Reinhold was all for pushing on, solo if need be; however, there was dissension

NANGA PARBAT 8125m

RUPAL FACE

—— *Messner Direct 1970*   — — *Polish Spur 1985*

Right The Southeast (Polish) Spur of Nanga Parbat in the upper part of Great Couloir. Severe mixed ground can be seen beyond the climber.

THE MESSNER SOLO OF THE DIAMIR FACE OF NANGA PARBAT

DIAMIR FACE, NANGA PARBAT.

After the Rupal Face, Reinhold Messner endured a trying period. He struggled through lawsuits with Herrligkoffer for breach of contract and libel (much as Buhl had had to do before him). In 1971, he met Uschi von Kielin, his one-time sponsor's wife, whom he later married. Together they returned to the Diamir Valley to try to find Günther's body, to no avail.

In 1972 he climbed Manaslu (8156m; 26,760ft), his second 8000m peak. On the way to the summit his partner, Franz Jager, turned back. Messner summitted alone. He made it back to the high camp in a storm, only to find Jager missing. Two climbers from Camp IV set out to find him, and one of these also lost his life. Messner went through a period of depression and then contemplation, which he came out of determined to climb a full 8000m peak solo — the obvious choice was Nanga Parbat: the Diamir Face, the magnet. In 1973 he attempted this, but could not complete it. 'I am not mentally ready yet to see such a big undertaking through to the end.' (Messner, The Challenge.)

In 1975 he joined the huge Italian siege on the South Face of Lhotse. He wrote: 'It is much easier to find a single well-matched partner than ten or fifteen.' (Ibid.) Soon he and Peter Habeler, an Austrian guide, were off on their alpine-style ascent of the 1200m (3937ft) Northwest Face of Hidden Peak (Gasherbrum 1 — 8068m; 26,470ft). They succeeded, setting new standards for 8000m ascents. In 1978, tagging onto an Austrian expedition, the pair reached the summit of Everest without using any oxygen on 8 May, giving lie to the debate then raging as to whether the human body and mind could survive this. For Messner it was a triumph, fitting in with his philosophy of reducing technical aids to the minimum.

In June of the same year Messner and Ursula Grether, a medical student, set out on his next attempt on Nanga Parbat. (His first marriage had broken up in 1977.) Messner considered the Diamir Face to be his greatest challenge. After two weeks at base camp, he felt ready for the 3500m (11,500ft) of face above him. His 15kg (33lb) pack contained the bare minimum for 4–5 days on the face: a tent, stove, food and sleeping bag. Via the Mummery Rib he gained height; on the second day he gained 1600m (5250ft) in six hours. Overnight a huge avalanche swept the entire face clean, just missing him and passing over his previous day's tracks. The next day brought him 1000m (3281ft) higher, to the base of the summit pyramid. The final day, carrying only his ice axe and camera, he made his way to the top. Negotiating snow-filled gullies and rocky steps, tiptoeing on crampon points at the limit of his endurance, only willpower kept him going. Suddenly, at 16:00, there was nothing more to climb.

Messner made it down safely in what turned out to be a race against a storm — he abandoned his tent, sleeping bag and all the equipment except his camera in a desperate downhill marathon, slipping, falling down avalanche-prone slopes, constantly on the edge of disaster. The first solo ascent of a full major Himalayan peak had been completed.

with Herrligkoffer. They agreed that, in the event of good weather, the three would fix ropes as high as possible for a combined summit bid by Felix Kuen, Peter Scholtz, Günther and Reinhold. If the weather was threatening, Reinhold, despite the protests of Herrligkoffer, would attempt a fast solo. The signal was a rocket to be fired from base camp – red for bad weather, blue for good. As fate would have it, the red rocket was encased in a blue cover, thus the 'good' weather forecast was twisted into 'bad' with the firing of a red rocket!

This led Reinhold Messner to decide on his solo summit bid, and he left at 03:00 for his Hermann Buhl-style attempt. After confusion in finding the route, he dropped back down a few hundred feet, and to his amazement he saw a figure moving up rapidly towards him. It was Günther, unable to resist a go at the summit. In only four hours, Günther had covered ground that would take Scholtz and Kuen over 10 hours the next day.

The brothers plugged on through the blisteringly hot day, and in the late afternoon they reached the summit. After the elation had subsided, reality set in. They had no rope, stove, food or liquids; their entire bivouac gear consisted of a paper-thin space blanket. To return down the Rupal route and Merkl Gully was impossible; they therefore decided to try the less steep Diamir Face, although neither knew it. Climbing to just below the summit pyramid, they huddled together, shivering all night.

The next day they could see Kuen and Scholz climbing up around the corner on the Rupal Face. All the brothers needed was a rope, but bad communication in the wind led the potential rescuers to believe they were fine. They waved cheerily, and went on to their own summit experience.

An exhausted Reinhold and his brother descended the 50-degree ice slopes to the comparative safety of Mummery Rib, which they reached at midnight. Setting out again before dawn, they pushed downwards, reaching the glacier as the sun rose. The pair, despite their exhaustion, congratulated each other on their double first – the Rupal Face, and the first traverse of Nanga Parbat. Dazed, they wandered down the

Above right Reinhold Messner, the first climber to summit every one of the 8000m peaks.

glacier, Reinhold in front, Günther behind, stopping to drink from rivulets of melted ice. Reinhold fell asleep while sipping water from a small pool. When he awoke, he looked for his brother. There was no sign of him.

Thereafter followed days of hell. He forced himself back up the glacier, shouting as best he was able. The sad truth dawned as he saw the debris of an ice avalanche that had swept across their tracks. He searched frantically for two days, tearing at the ice, shouting until he could not

even whisper. At last he had to admit the worst, and for three more days and nights he staggered like a drunk towards the valley below until he stumbled into the grazing camp of the local villagers. He had not eaten for a week, had spent a night at over 8000m (26,000ft), and lost his brother. Despite all this, and also the subsequent loss of some of his toes, Reinhold's will to overcome has led him on to many challenges – not the least his record of being the first to surmount all 14 of the 8000m peaks.

HIGH-ALTITUDE PEAKS

HIGH-ALTITUDE PEAKS

THE OGRE • ACONCAGUA • MOUNT McKINLEY • KILIMANJARO • MOUNT KENYA

The fourteen 8000m (26,000ft) peaks are not the only ones worthy of mention as high-altitude mountains – after all, the 8000m line is arbitrary – why not 7500m (24,600ft), or 7000m (23,000ft)? The difficulty or beauty of a climb is made up of many factors other than altitude, though it does have an important effect. Anything above 5000m (16,400ft) can be considered high enough to cause altitude-related problems.

Among the peaks chosen here, one is a 7000+m (23,000+ft) Himalayan peak, and the rest represent the highest in various other areas of the world, but all above the 5000m (16,400ft) mark. Some of these mountains succumbed easily, others only after a struggle, but all offer superbly challenging climbing on one or another of their many routes.

The difficulties in high-altitude climbing are the effects of altitude, weather, access and unstable snow and ice. High mountains tend to be subject to abrupt variations in weather, and climbers sometimes wait for weeks for a break in the weather, only to be rebuffed in their attempts by another spell of poor conditions. High-altitude mountaineering takes a special breed of person – a combination of aggressive determination, stoic patience, fearlessness tempered with caution, careful planning and the ability to make snap decisions.

The large expeditions of yesteryear have largely given way to lightweight, alpine-style pushes. This is in no small measure due to the advances in equipment. Miracle fabrics such as Gore-Tex, and refinements in plastics, carbon-fibre and metals have given rise to warm- and wet-weather equip-ment that weighs a fraction of the older materials. Prepackaged, high-energy food, more efficient stoves, single-skin tents, and a host of other tech-nological developments have gone hand-in-hand with improved fitness training and a mental out-look that encourages fast ascents without oxygen. The modern climber has more reliable, efficient and lighter kit than that of his predecessors.

Rather than allowing this to make life easier, the cutting-edge climbers keep the levels of challenge on a par with those of earlier climbers by attempt-ing more difficult unclimbed peaks, forging harder and steeper variations to previously climbed sum-mits, climbing solo, doing winter ascents, or de-creasing the time taken to climb. New routes are being put up virtually daily in the Andes of South America, the Pamirs, the Karakoram (Trango Towers, Shipton Spire, Mustagh Tower, Latok and Chogolisa) and other areas of the Himalayas.

A recent noteworthy feat is that of Vanja Furlan and Tomaz Humar of Slovenia with their five-day alpine-style ascent of the 1650m (5400ft) North-west Face of the 6856m (22,494ft) Ama Dablam (Nepal Himalaya), including an unprotected solo of most of a 1200ft (3937m) ice wall at 80 degrees – after accidentally dropping all their ice protection!

Other feats include speed records, such as the official one on Khan Tegri (6995m; 23,000ft) in Kirghizstan, held by Alex Lowe, USA, standing at 10 hours, 13 minutes. This is the peak where the outstanding Soviet mountaineer, Vitali Abalakov, lost most of his fingers and toes from frostbite in 1936, at the end of his six-day ascent.

THE OGRE
Location: Karakoram
Summit height: 7272m (23,900ft)
First ascent: West Ridge – Chris Bonington, Doug Scott (UK), 1977

ACONCAGUA
Location: Central Andes, South America
Summit height: 6962m (22,840ft)
First ascent: West Flank – Matthias Zurbriggen (Swiss), solo, 14 January 1897

MOUNT McKINLEY
Location: Alaska Range, North America
Summit height: 6193m (20,319ft)
First ascent: North Summit – Peter Anderson and Billy Taylor (Sourdough Expedition), April 1910; South Summit – Harry Karstens, Reverend Hudson Stuck, Walter Harper, Robert Tatum, 7 June 1913

KILIMANJARO
Location: Kenya–Tanzania border, East Africa
Summit height: 5895m (19,341ft)
First ascent: Kibo – Hans Meyer and Ludwig Purtscheller, 1889; Breach Wall – Reinhold Messner (Italy) with Konrad Renzler, 1978

MOUNT KENYA
Location: Kenya, East Africa
Summit height: 5199m (17,058ft)
First ascent: Batian – Halford McKinder with C Ollier and J Brocherel, 1899; Nelion – Eric Shipton and Percy Wyn Harris, 1929; Diamond Couloir – Phil Snyder with Thumbe Matenge, 1973

Previous pages Approaching the rock tower leading to the summit of The Ogre on the West Ridge route.
Opposite Looking over Kahiltna Glacier from 5500m (18,045ft) on the West Rib of Denali, McKinley Range.
Top right A mountaineer trudges up the steep West Ridge route of The Ogre between camps IV and V.

The Ogre

Baintha Brakk – A Symphony of Pain and Pleasure

'To regain the peg crack, I had to push myself well over to the left as I abseiled. I stepped my right foot up against the wall, but in the gathering darkness, unwittingly placed it on a veneer of water ice. Suddenly my foot shot off, and I found myself swinging away into the gloom, clutching the end of the rope. I slammed into the opposite side of the gully, 100 feet away. Splat! Glasses gone, and every bone shaken … So, that's how it was going to be, a whole new game, with new restrictions on winning.' (Doug Scott, *A Crawl Down The Ogre*.)

Many accidents happen in climbing, but few in as isolated and life-threatening a situation as the one Doug Scott describes above. This was not on some little local crag, with a rescue helicopter and hospital around the corner. This swing, which broke Scott's right leg and left ankle, happened at the top of the 7272m (23,900ft) Ogre, in the isolated wilds of the Karakoram. It was an unfortunate way to end what had been a stupendous climb.

In the centre of the unforgiving landscape of the Karakoram, the Uzum Brakk Glacier swings in a gigantic sickle to the base of the Ogre–Latok group. Matthew Dickinson, on the recent British Ogre–Latok Expedition, wrote: 'The Ogre presides at the foot of the glacier, its sheer array of golden granite making it a stunning sight.'

In 1977, an expedition arrived to challenge this awesome giant. It was a British group of mountaineers with enviable reputations: Mo Anthoine, Paul Braithwaite, Clive Rowland, Nick Estcourt,

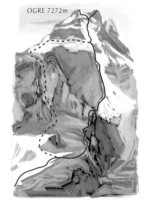

--- *Western Spur (Bonington) 1970*
— *Central Spur (Bonington) 1970*

Chris Bonington and Doug Scott – as powerful a group of climbers as one could imagine. The Ogre had defeated many previous attempts – beaten the climbers back with its combination of incredibly sustained steep rock and ice on all sides, extreme weather and remoteness. The first attempt on the Central Spur ended when Scott accidentally knocked a large rock down, dislocating Braithwaite's hip. The other four were meanwhile pushing on up the steep rock and ice to the left of this central pillar, and succeeded in getting to the Western Col. Bonington and Estcourt shot onwards to attempt the main summit, but a lack of food and equipment, combined with Estcourt succumbing to a throat infection (a common problem at altitude), led to their settling for the lower West Summit.

Two days later, Scott, Bonington, Anthoine and Rowland set off for the main summit. They followed the path set up by the earlier pair via the 'mixed' (snow, rock and ice) rib to the left of the Central Spur onto the rock towers leading to the West Summit, and then via an abseil to a bivouac on the col between the West and Main summits. The next morning they set off, but Anthoine and Rowland retreated once they saw that the others were going very slowly on the main tower. This was a steep and unrelenting 250m (820ft) piece of rock, on which Bonington led the first hard pitch at Grade IV, and later Scott the much longer, more serious crux pitch at Grade VI/A2. Doug Scott rated it as 'the hardest climbing I've ever done at

Top left Clive Rowland and Mo Anthoine on the upper part of the West Ridge, with no margin for error.
Centre left The view from Camp IV down the Uzum Brakk Glacier is breathtaking in its height and beauty.
Bottom left Chris Bonington is dwarfed by the size of the Summit Tower, South Face, The Ogre, in 1977.
Opposite Clouds stream from the twin summits of The Ogre, as seen from the distant Hispar Saddle.

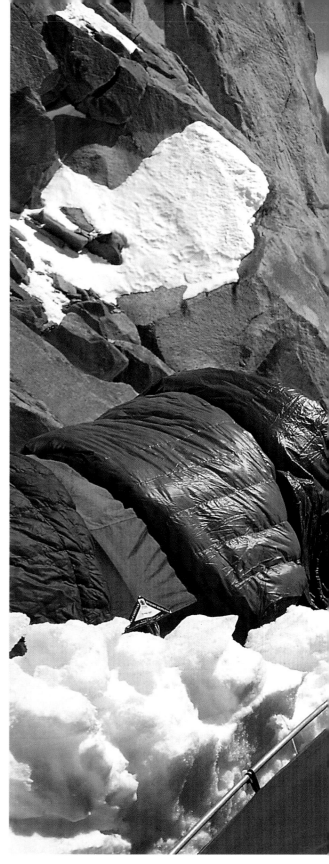

altitude' – which is quite a statement coming from such a strong climber! 'Combined tactics' (Scott standing on Bonington's back to reach over an overhang) led to the final snow gully and the summit. In Doug Scott's words: 'I reached the top just as the sun disappeared below the horizon. As Chris followed, I had time to enjoy just being up there in the middle of the Karakoram, surrounded by glaciers and other granite peaks as far as the eye could see. But even as the first superlatives were

flowing out of Chris' mouth, I was hustling to get us down before it was totally dark. We had no sleeping bags and only very light clothing under our wind suits. A forced bivouac held no attractions.'

Soon after this their seven-day descent began, with Doug Scott slamming into the wall and breaking a leg and an ankle. This brought about an enforced, bitterly cold high bivouac, followed by two days of blizzards which pinned the group in the snow cave on the col. Then came Scott's amazing

Top left Steep ice gives way to even steeper rock on The Ogre between camps IV and V.

Left A lengthy string of porters ferrying essential supplies to base camp.

Above The view from Camp IV. Some of the minor peaks in view have yet to receive a first ascent.

descent, supported by Bonington and the others, which entailed agonizing abseils, and hundreds of metres of crawling across snow fields, as well as hauling himself up ropes to the West Summit. At one point Bonington abseiled off the end of a rope and broke a number of ribs (which later caused him to contract pneumonia). Scott crawled the last 4.8km (3 miles) down the glacier on his own, the

rest having gone ahead to organize stretcher bearers and recall the others who had gone to arrange a search party. The group, aided by Balti porters, carried Scott out to Askole where a helicopter could pick him up. This got as far as Skardu, then crash-landed, fortunately with no injuries, but leaving the weakened Bonington to make his way out on foot. The party had won, but nearly at the cost of a life.

The Ogre, which still awaits a second ascent, holds many challenges for climbers, not the least being the as-yet-unclimbed Southeast Pillar, which has tempted over 10 expeditions. The route is littered with abandoned gear and abseil points, particularly on the lower reaches of its 1000m (3300ft) of rock. The final 400m (1300ft) summit tower which caps the route has yet to be ascended.

Aconcagua

The Penitent Zone

Aconcagua holds the distinction of being the highest mountain in the western and southern hemispheres. It has a rich history, starting with its first attempt in an incredible fashion in 1883 by Professor Paul Güssfeldt of Berlin University. With no companions other than three Chilean mule drivers, or *huasos*, this bold soul approached Aconcagua from the north. With no tent and only one thin sleeping bag among the four, he persuaded the drivers to accompany him up the 1000m (3000ft) rock wall, which he called the Sierra delle Penitente, to a gap called the Bussertor, at 5025m (16,500ft), where he made camp. Frostbite and altitude sickness depleted his party one by one. After three days (which included two nights of nonstop climbing), Güssfeldt and one *huaso* retreated after reaching 6550m (21,500ft) – only 500m (1500ft) short of the summit (probably a world altitude record for the time). Despite many subsequent attempts, his route was not completed until an Austro-German expedition finally climbed it in 1951.

In December 1896 the wealthy dilettante Englishman, Edward Fitzgerald – accompanied by his long-time Swiss guide, Matthias Zurbriggen, and five Swiss and Italian porters – arrived at the western side, the Horcones Glacier. The pair had made several important ascents in New Zealand, the Andes and the Alps, and Fitzgerald was himself a solid climber. The otherwise well-organized expedition almost foundered because

ACONCAGUA 6962m

— — French Route 1954
——— Argentinian Route 1966

of faulty stoves, and they eventually had to rely on wood to cook their meals (described by Zurbriggen as 'indigestible rubbish', to Fitzgerald's chagrin as he had carefully worked them out). They somehow managed to make a fire at 6645m (21,800ft) – quite an amazing feat. At this point a bottle of champagne exploded because of low pressure, 'which discouraged us greatly', Fitzgerald later wrote. This halt, called to boil water, possibly intensified Fitzgerald's altitude sickness and he was forced to descend, frustrated and disappointed. Zurbriggen kept on going alone, plodding through the loose, rolling stones which are the curse of all Aconcagua climbers, and reached the summit at 16:45. He made it back to the 5700m (18,700ft) camp at 22:00, exhausted and mildly frostbitten, in the typical high wind which characterizes the weather on this mountain.

In 1898, on what could have been the second full ascent of Aconcagua, Martin Conway, a rival of Fitzgerald, stopped his team a mere 100m (328ft) below the summit – he then publicly gave out the knowledge that 'he did this so as not to insult Fitzgerald, who had taken two months to accomplish what he had done in only one week'. This did not impress Fitzgerald, who was in the process of publishing a dramatic book on Andean climbing, out of which he hoped to make quite a sizable revenue. Soon after this Fitzgerald gave up all climbing.

Opposite In earlier days this approach to the East Face of Aconcagua necessitated a 38km (24-mile) walk-in.
Top right Climbers at 6850m (22,475ft) approaching the final snow-covered section of Aconcagua.
Bottom right Camp II after a snowfall. Aconcagua's erratic weather has confounded many an attempt.

The ordinary route, via the Horcones Glacier and Western Flank, is regarded today as 'easy' and climbed by many hundreds of mountaineers each year. It is still not a safe peak – no peak of this magnitude can ever be considered 'safe' and scores of lives are lost each year (over 70 lives have been lost on this route to date). The combination of high winds (up to 200kph; 160mph), sudden storms, extreme dry cold (as low as –45°C; –49°F) and altitude take their toll. This occurs particularly among inexperienced climbers who ascend too fast up the long standard route, or who spend too long in the high-altitude huts at over 6095m (20,000ft).

ACONCAGUA SOUTH FACE

The giant South Face of Aconcagua plummets for a near-vertical 3000m (10,000ft) from the summit to the Horcones Glacier far below. In 1952 the French alpinists Lionel Terray and Guido Magnone first saw this impressive face, and recognized it as 'the greatest problem outside the Himalayas'. This proclamation came to the attention of René Ferlet, who put together a small group of French climbers to confirm Terray's judgement. Lucien Bernadini, Adrein Dagory, Edmond Denis, Pierre Lasueur, Robert Paragot and Guy Poulet accompanied him to South America. To avoid the dangers of avalanches and falling ice, they chose to attack the great Central Pillar. Climbing in relays, the team surmounted the difficult and

technically challenging broken rock and ice at the start, fixing ropes to make load-carrying easier and safer. This section includes Grade VI climbing – no mean feat at this altitude.

A high camp was established above the initial buttresses, and then the group tackled the huge ice

Right Cloud formations over Aconcagua. The 'false' summit is created by the powerful winds that are the nemesis of climbers.

fields above this camp. Fighting the vagaries of the weather, they proceeded cautiously, with constant up-and-down movement, through the excellent rock of the sandstone girdle in the middle of the face, to establish a high bivouac camp. Finally the team pushed up the top rock band, a vertical and solid rampart, then over a huge, steep ice bulge and through the icy exit ramps. Most of the climbing was very boldly done in alpine style (no porters or tents, and thus little load-ferrying). It took a further three cold, uncomfortable bivouacs before the group finally stood on the summit. Six of them 'topped out' (Ferlet just didn't make it to the summit). All seven members of the team suffered from fairly serious frostbite. It took close on a month for the team to achieve the summit, but they succeeded in establishing what is regarded as one of the most challenging routes in the Andes, described by Messner as follows: 'For the modern top climber it represents an adventure, a mountaineering achievement, and an experience worthy of profound respect.' The South Face route still lures many climbers each year, and is often used as a 'training ground' for the Himalayan giants.

Above The South Face of Aconcagua, showing the vast scale and steep aspect of the face.

Below left A party at 6400m (21,000ft) – 500m (1640ft) short of the summit, with a long day ahead.

Below A climber perches uneasily in his high bivouac on the South Face of Aconcagua.

Mount McKinley

Denali – Home of the Midnight Sun

Mountaineering, politics and money seem to be odd bedfellows, yet in the case of Mount McKinley, in Alaska, the three became closely associated. In the late 1800s, the Dominion of Canada was forged and the Canadian Pacific Railroad established. This needed some economic justification other than pure exploration, thus the Canadian Mountains were promulgated as the 'New Alps', and the famous Edward Whymper, among others, was given all-expenses-paid holidays to climb the peaks on the promise of writing and lecturing about them afterwards. This had the desired effect, although it was mostly the peaks close to civilization that were climbed.

In 1897, W A Dickey, a surveyor and prospector, came to within 160km (100 miles) of McKinley, sketched it, and wrote of its 'great height', guessing it to be 7000m (23,000ft). He found its Indian name to be Denali – 'the Great One', or 'Home of the Sun' – but named it Mount McKinley to honour American president William McKinley. Since the peak was actually in Alaska, the Canadian authorities protested, insisting that Mount Robson (only 3950m; 12,972ft) was the highest peak in the north (it was then Canada's highest peak, and was not itself conquered until 1913). The border between Canada and Alaska was later altered, placing Mount Logan (6050m; 19,850ft) in Canada! In 1903 Judge James Wickersham led his McKinley expedition to 3050m (10,000ft) on the Wickersham Wall, and established that the peak was 'considerably higher than Robson'. In the same year, Dr Frederick Cook

made his first trip to the mountain. In 1906 he was back with a large party, but months of siege brought them no success and the team dispersed. When they reunited, Cook announced that he and Edward Barille had 'conquered the highest peak on the Continent'. The photograph he was displaying proved to be a fake, and the claim was discredited.

SOUTH PEAK
6193m

NORTH PEAK
5934m

——— Muldrow & Harper Glacier 1910
- - - Pioneer Ridge 1961
····· Wickersham Wall Canadian 1963
— — Integral Route 1988

Despite this setback, he was well paid for his lectures and for writing *To the Top of the Continent*. It is unfortunate that Cook demeaned himself, as his exploits were remarkable, without having to falsely claim the prizes he desired.

The controversy over McKinley brought about one of the most amazing expeditions ever. A group of miners and trappers in Fairbanks, Alaska, led by Tom Lloyd and Billy Taylor, accepted the local innkeeper's challenge to scale the peak before 4 July 1910 'to show that ponce [presumably Cook] who's boss' – and for the US$5000 prize, no doubt! The Sourdough Expedition (a name derived from the miners' hard bread), left Fairbanks just before Christmas 1909. Using dog sleds, they traversed McGonagall Pass to the Muldrow Glacier. Eleven weeks later they made camp at 3350m (11,000ft), at the end of the glacier. They had made their own axes and crampons, and armed with these they attacked the ridge now known as Karstens Ridge. They cut nearly 1.5km (1 mile) of steps, then, with Tom Lloyd, Charley McGonagall and two other sourdoughs out of the race, Peter Anderson and Billy Taylor dashed for the summit. This meant a rise of 2600m (8530ft) up deep snow fields, hampered by

Opposite Mount McKinley from the south – the South Ridge tending down right from the South Summit.
Top left This long line of climbers is headed towards the fixed lines to the crest of the West Buttress.
Bottom left Modern capsule-style climbing usually involves a good deal of personal load-carrying.

a 4m (14ft) fir flagpole on which they later hung the Stars and Stripes. Believing it to be the highest, they went for, and made, the 'lesser' North Summit (5934m; 19,469ft) – still no mean achievement!

Their claim was discredited for years, as Lloyd and Taylor had sounded unbelievable. Taylor also claimed that they had climbed both summits.

In 1912 Professor Herschel Parker (who had been on Cook's expedition), Belmore Browne and Merl la Voy (who had turned back on the original Sourdough Expedition), with newcomer Arthur Aten, followed the Sourdough route but branched off to the south. They made it to within literally a score of metres of the South Summit, at 5880m (19,300ft), when a violent storm compelled them to descend. A few days later they tried again, but once again retreated at about the same height in the teeth of a gale-force blizzard. They proved their claim with descriptions and diagrams, and the very

act of denying themselves the glory of claiming the summit brought some relief to the somewhat scandalized Mount McKinley climbing scene.

Browne wrote: 'My sleeping bag weighed seventeen pounds. It was large, and made of the best blue wolf fur. Professor Parker dressed more warmly than either La Voy or myself. He wore at night a complete suit of double llama wool beside his mountain clothing, and yet he could not sleep for the cold.' A far cry from today's superdown, Gore-Tex-lined bags and fleece suits!

In 1913 four more experienced climbers – Harry Karstens (a prospector and adventurer), Rev Hudson Stuck (who described himself as a 'muscular Christian'), Walter Harper (an Alaskan Indian), and Robert Tatum (a young missionary) – headed for McKinley. They, too, ascended via McGonagall Pass, up the long Muldrow Glacier and then the Karstens Ridge. The well-organized and well-

equipped group made rapid progress up the now-familiar territory, reaching the South Summit, at 6193m (20,319ft) the highest point in North America, on 7 June 1913. From here the tattered flagpole on the North Summit was clearly visible – the Sourdough Expedition was vindicated at last!

The accomplishment of these climbers should not be taken lightly – McKinley's height of just over 6000m (22,000ft) is deceptive. From the surrounding plateau to the summit involves a rise of over 5200m (17,000ft) as compared to Everest, which has a rise of 3960m (13,000ft), albeit at a greater altitude.

In 1951 Bradford Washburn, one of the leading mountain photographers in the world, climbed the elegant West Buttress route, now the most popular route on the peak, being the shortest, safest and easiest. From Washburn's pictures sprang a fresh interest in Mount McKinley.

THE SOUTH FACE ROUTE

Italian Riccardo Cassin is regarded as one of the finest climbers of the century. He and his team flew in to the Kahiltna Glacier, where they established base at 3200m (10,500ft) on 2 July 1961. Their route followed the long central ridge, with Grade IV climbing on the slabby granite. This was followed by a gully at Grade V. The party faced constant bad weather, with gale force winds and the sight of sun a rarity. Three weeks of effort brought them to the summit at 23:00 on 19 July, after 16 hours without food or rest. After a few minutes' rest, they started back, but Canali became disorientated, slipped regularly, and had to be held by Cassin. Eventually the group reached their tiny tents in the pitch dark, as much by luck as by judgement.

Opposite Viewed from 4877m (16,000ft): East Kahiltna Peak (right) and Mount Hunter beyond.

Above Fixed ropes at 4877m (16,000ft) make the West Buttress a climb with an expeditionary nature.

Right Mario Bilodeau and Mark Whiton at the 'top of North America' – the summit of McKinley.

The route was 3050m (10,000ft) long, at an average angle of 50 degrees. It was heralded as the climb of the decade, and is still held in awe by mountaineers. Fosco Maraini wrote of Cassin in the *Alpine Journal*: 'One must not forget that Cassin was fifty-three at the time. There is something indestructible about this man. I can just see

Riccardo snuffing his way up the crags and ice of McKinley in the horrid subarctic gales, like an old bear who plays a difficult and drawn-out game with the gods of darkness and cold, of loneliness and hunger, knowing quite well that they might be powerful, but that he is tougher, keener, shrewder than all of them put together.'

Kilimanjaro

Kibo — an African Experience

When European traders reached the shores of East Africa, they heard of a high mountain crowned with silver. The whole place was so full of *djinn* (bad spirits) that any who tried to climb it died, their legs and arms stiff and blackened – a testimony to the effects of frostbite.

The highest point in Africa, Mount Kilimanjaro (Kibo) in Tanzania, is a dormant volcano, one of the largest in the world. It rears eerily above the plains of the Masai Steppe, which teem with wildlife in strange contrast to the glittering snows above. It rises 4500m (15,000ft) out of the plains to a huge, mildly conical top of over 5km² (2½ sq. miles).

In 1889 Leipzig geographer Hans Meyer, accompanied by Austrian guide Ludwig Purtscheller and Tanzanian Y Louwa, crossed the plateau, stopping to hunt along the way. They made their way up the saddle and the southern rim to the summit peak, which they called the Kaiser Wilhelm Spitze. (The Kenyan authorities in 1961 renamed it Uhuru Peak – Kilimanjaro straddles the Kenyan border with Tanzania.) The original route is now called the Marangu route, and is equipped with huts. Altitude sickness takes a heavy toll of its ascendants as a result of the rapid rate of rise from the plateau.

Kilimanjaro has many fine routes, including the Western Breach Umbwe route of 1963 – no more than a scramble, but an excellent one; and the Heim route, a fine, moderate ice climb next to the 1200m (4000ft) Southern Breach Wall. Ian Howell (UK) put up many superb routes on Kilimanjaro,

KIBO 5895m

—— *Original Route 1957*
- - - *Kersten Glacier Direct Route 1975*
· · · · · *Breach Wall: Balletto Ice Field 1975*
— — *Breach Wall Direct (Messner) 1978*

including the Direct on the Kersten Glacier (with O'Connor and Cleare in 1975) – a line up the centre of the glacier, involving Grade VI/A1 ice with a precarious hanging bivouac.

THE GREAT BREACH WALL

This is one of Africa's major mountaineering problems. The main wall looms for thousands of feet, the upper reaches dominated by huge permanent 'icicles' hanging from the top of Diamond Glacier. The scale is Himalayan, with long nights, high altitude and extreme cold combining to make this a unique African experience.

John Temple, with Tony Charlton in 1975 and with Dave Cheesemond in 1976, forged two difficult lines up the Breach Wall, starting with the lower tier of mixed ground, up hundreds of metres of vertical rock to the steep Balletto Icefield, and on to the near-vertical upper tier of hanging ice and rock. These were excellent routes, but both avoided the 160m (500ft) Breach Wall Icicle that links the Balletto Icefield with the Diamond Glacier – which tempted and defeated climbers for over a decade.

In 1978 the legendary Reinhold Messner came to have a look at the Last Great African Challenge, as the icicle was called. True to form, he managed to complete the Breach route from bottom to top in just two days, including the elusive Great Breach Wall Icicle – perhaps a small feat for the man who, in that same year, ascended Everest without oxygen and soloed Nanga Parbat.

Opposite Elephants of the Amboseli National Park are overshadowed by the imposing bulk of Kibo.
Top right A view over Balletto Glacier to the Great Breach Wall Icicle trickling from the Diamond Glacier.
Centre right The Kersten Glacier Direct first ascent; Bill O'Connor leads a vertical ice pitch on Snout Wall.
Bottom right Some unusual load-carrying as this party leaves the moorland zone on the Marangu route.

Mount Kenya

The Bright Mountain

In 1849 a Lutheran missionary, Dr Johan Krapf, brought reports to Europe of 'immense snow-covered mountains in the centre of Africa' which he had seen from miles away across the plateau. He was ridiculed by 'experts' such as Sir Desmond Cowley, an eminent geographer who never ventured further abroad than his armchair at the Royal Geographical Society! But when German explorer Count von Szek reached the mountain in 1876 and climbed to 4510m (14,800ft), his stories were so well supported that Dr Krapf was finally vindicated.

In 1899 Sir Halford McKinder led a large party to the mountain. After many attempts, he and two guides finally found a route to the summit of Batian – crossing the South and Southeast faces of Nelion and cutting up the high-level Diamond Glacier (not to be confused with that of the same name on Kilimanjaro) to the final rock ridge. McKinder named the three highest summits Batian, Nelion and Lenana after three of the Maasai's last great *laibons* – seers and medicine men who ruled the tribe.

Nelion was not to see a successful ascent for 30 years, when the renowned Eric Shipton and Percy Wyn Harris climbed the Southeast Face, a Grade III climb on verglassed rock (*see* page 159). The next year Shipton, with Bill Tilman, scaled the steep Northwest Ridge, starting at the Firmin Col.

Another historical climb that brought fame to the peak is recorded in *No Picnic on Mount Kenya* (Felice Benuzzi) – the tale of the three Italian prisoners of war who in 1943 escaped from their

BATIAN 5199m NELION 5188m

- - - - - *Normal Route 1929*
———— *South Face Route 1950*
— — *Diamond Couloir 1973*
- - - *Diamond Buttress 1976*

prison in the foothills 48km (30 miles) away with the sole intention of climbing Mount Kenya. They were: Felice Benuzzi, a seasoned mountaineer who had grown up in the Italian Dolomites, Giovanni Baletto, another ex-Dolomite climber, and Enzo Barsotti, a nonclimber who simply wanted to 'be there.' For a year they scrounged food and blankets, made clothes from scraps, fashioned crampons and axes from cans, and made ropes from bed netting. On 24 January they sneaked out and made their gruelling way through the wild African bush, having to avoid not only people but also elephant, leopard and buffalo. They finally reached Batian's Northwest Ridge and, after a heroic attempt, were driven off by blizzards and their own deteriorating state as a result of lack of proper food and clothing. Despite limited equipment and food, they succeeded in climbing as far as McKinder's earlier attempt, and also in ascending to the summit of the 4985m (16,355ft) Lenana.

They returned and surrendered to a mystified camp warden, who waived most of their punishment in appreciation of their sporting effort.

THE DIAMOND COULOIR

Mount Kenya is surrounded by a cluster of satellite pinnacles and 15 glaciers. The largest and steepest of these is the Diamond Glacier, which hangs down on the south side of the Gate of the Mist (the icy gash that separates Batian and Nelion). From its fearsome snout a vertical 370m (1200ft) ice

Top left Nelion (left) and Batian stand proud over the (sadly) diminishing Diamond Glacier of Mount Kenya.
Centre left A climber on Mount Kenya stands in front of a gigantic ice cave, with its sword-like stalactites.
Bottom left Making use of a rock feature, this climber takes a break on an abseil descent from the summit.
Opposite Batian and Nelion, the twin summits of Mount Kenya, with Point John Spire visible to their right.

gully drops in a few jagged steps to the Darwin Glacier. This is the Diamond Couloir, long admired by mountaineers but considered suicidal because of the overhanging snout of the Diamond Glacier and the narrow, enclosing walls which channel any avalanches and icefall directly onto climbers, leaving them no chance of escape. This most spectacular route, and one of the few worthwhile semi-permanent ice climbs in Africa, goes through this hazardous gully. Any pebble or chunk of ice on the whole southwestern cirque of the mountain will end up spinning down this couloir.

In 1971, Ian 'Pin' Howell and Phil Snyder, an American who ran the Kenyan National Park, managed to find a route through the lower reaches, but could not finish the climb before the African night set in. The next day poor weather caused them to abort their attempts, and a sudden end to the short 'winter' put off further climbs on the now-melting icefall. Pin was back the next year, with John Cleare, a British ice climber. Twice they mastered the 50m (150ft) vertical ice pillar but had to retreat. Here is Cleare's description, from his book *Mountains*: 'Dawn in Africa comes fast and it is suddenly light as we strap on our crampons and start up the steep ice of the Darwin towards the dark gash of the couloir ahead. But today the light is dead. I am reminded more of Ben Nevis on a bad November day than the Equator in August.' And later: 'I am on the sharp end of the rope, and I'm a long way out from the stance. There's no problem with route finding – it's just straight up. Another couple of moves and I can stick my foot out onto that little snow-covered nick on the rock wall. I bridge wide, and lean forward with relief. Totally engrossed in the problem of surmounting the Glass Wall there is no longer room in my mind for fear.' They did not, unfortunately, complete the climb.

It was then Snyder's turn and, in the absence of another experienced climber, he persuaded a local ranger, Thumbe Matenge, to accompany him. This must have been quite an initiation for Matenge, but showing great determination, he managed to belay and follow Snyder up the steep, hard ice to the top of the ice pillar in the couloir. This led them to an ice cave – the jaws of the Diamond – and they made their way through the dark tunnel with its icicles hanging like proverbial Swords of Damocles. It gave on to an ill-protected ice-rock chimney that brought them out above the snout. A few easy pitches up the Diamond Glacier led them through the Gate of the Mist. The Grade VI 'Glass Wall Game' had been completed.

The American Yvon Chouinard, of Yosemite fame, added a direct finish up and over the huge ice snout in 1975 to complete the aesthetic beauty of the direct line up the Diamond from bottom to top.

Opposite The Diamond Couloir – a spectacular but dangerous funnel of constant avalanches.

Below McKinder's Camp in the Teleki Valley.

ALPINE-SCALE PEAKS

ALPINE-SCALE PEAKS

MONT BLANC • THE MATTERHORN • THE EIGER • THE PETIT DRU • MOUNT COOK

The concept of alpinism is essentially that of climbing routes that involve both rock and snow or ice climbing – even if the latter two may only occur in approaching the climb over glaciers or snow slopes. Alpine-style ascents – carrying minimal bivouac equipment, and moving 'capsule-style', i.e. with no supporting sub-camps or porters – are now becoming accepted as the way to go on many giant peaks previously climbed 'expedition' or 'siege'-style.

Alpine climbing is usually undertaken on peaks of a fair height, both in altitude and route length, and often involves long days of climbing and the necessity for bivouacs. Speed and sufficient competence on the part of all members of the party to move together over difficult terrain are hallmarks of successful alpine climbing.

Alpine climbing has had a long history of guiding, and many of the pioneers were referred to as amateurs, as opposed to their professional guides. The reality of the situation was that the amateurs were frequently as skilled as the guides, and some (such as Edward Whymper, William Coolidge, Geoffrey Winthrop-Young and the Duke of Abruzzi) were as proficient as the professionals.

Of the earlier Alpine guides, one of the most famous was Christian Almer (whose name even means 'of the Alps' – 'Alm' being the Swiss term for 'Alp'). Almer led a celebrated Wetterhorn climb from Grindelwald, guiding Sir Alfred Wills, a highly respected judge, whose evocative writing about the climb in *Wanderings Amongst the Alps* in 1854 is reputed to have contributed greatly to

the dawn of the 'Golden Age of Mountaineering'. This period, from December 1857 to World War I in 1914, saw the first (and many variation) ascents of all the major Alpine Peaks, as well as many summits around the globe. The effect of the earlier Alpine authors and photographers has been likened to 'the effect of modern-day pop stars on television in promoting fads and fancies'. Be that as it may, mountaineering had its 50-odd years of public adulation.

Christian Almer and his wife celebrated their golden wedding anniversary in 1896 (both were over 70) by climbing the Wetterhorn, with their five sons, all respected guides in their own right.

Names such as Michel Croz (France), Alex Burgener and Melchior Anderreg (Switzerland), and Laurent Croux and Jean-Antoine Carrel (Italy) are legendary in Alpine guiding, as are Joseph Knubel (Switzerland), Pierre Allain and Gaston Rébuffat (France), Fulgenzio Dimai and his twin sons, Angelo and Giuseppe, as well as Walter Bonatti (Italy), and Thomas Fyfe (New Zealand).

Guiding is no longer considered, as it once was, a virtual necessity, particularly by skilled climbers. Europe has thousands of registered, qualified guides, many of whom pioneer serious routes, sometimes with colleagues, on other occasions with competent clients, much as in the old days. Standards are high, and guides are still held in high regard by most mountaineers.

The breeding ground of Alpinism was the European Alps, and it is to these that we turn for descriptions of the Alpine experience.

MONT BLANC
Location: French Alps, Mont Blanc range
Summit height: 4807m (15,771ft)
First ascent: Peak – J Balmat, M Paccard (France), 8 August 1786; Central Pillar of Frêney – D Whillans, C Bonington, I Clough (UK), J Dlugosz (Polish), 1961

THE MATTERHORN
Location: Swiss-Italian Alps
Summit height: 4477m (14,690ft)
First ascent: Peak – E Whymper, C Hudson, Lord Francis Douglas, D Hadow (UK), M Croz (France), Peter and Peter (Jnr) Taugwalder (Swiss), 14 July 1865; North Face – Franz and Toni Schmid, 1931

THE EIGER
Location: Bernese Alps, Western Europe
Summit height: 3970m (13,026ft)
First ascent: Peak – C Barrington (UK), C Almer, P Bohren (Swiss), 11 August 1858; North Face – H Harrer (Austrian), F Kasparek, A Heckmair, L Vörg (German), 24 July 1938

THE PETIT DRU
Location: Mont Blanc range
Summit height: 3733m (12,248ft)
First ascent: Peak – C Dent, J Walker (UK), A Burgener, K Maurer (Swiss), 1878; South-west Pillar – W Bonatti (Italy), 1955

MOUNT COOK (AORANGI)
Location: Southern Alps, South Island, New Zealand
Summit height: 3754m (12,316ft)
First ascent: G Graham, T Fyfe, J Clarke (New Zealand), 25 December 1894

Previous pages A well-equipped climber approaching the summit of Mount Cook in early morning light.
Opposite The distinctive Matterhorn as it looks in summer, showing the Zmutt Ridge in the foreground.
Top right A climber silhouetted against Bolivian peaks – South America offers many Alpine-scale experiences.

Mont Blanc

The Top of Europe

Mont Blanc, the highest point in Western Europe, although currently regarded as a relatively easy climb, did not succumb readily. Jealously guarded on the southern and western (Italian) side by steep faces and rock walls, and by the mass of glaciers on the northern and eastern (French) sides, the top of the massif repelled many serious attempts in the mid-1700s. The gleaming white dome of the summit, easily visible from the valleys below, was a tempting and elusive prize, and in 1761, the attraction of summitting 'the Pole of Europe' was spiced by the large reward offered by the Genevan scientist, Horace-Benedict de Saussure. By 1785, despite the superstitions still attached to the high peaks, Chamonix explorers Jean-Marie Coutett, Francois Cuidet and Jacques Balmat had climbed as far as the Dome de Goûter as a team. Balmat became separated from the party, and was stranded overnight with no ill effects (until then, a high bivouac was deemed impossible, both because of the extreme cold and the mountain spirits). Balmat's return, unharmed, from his overnight stay was the talk of the valley.

MONT BLANC 4807m

—— *Original Route 1786*
— — *Grand Moulet Route 1859*
····· *Goûter Ridge 1861*
- - - *NE Ridge from Col du Midi 1863*

THE FIRST ASCENT

A Chamonix doctor, Michel Paccard, hearing of this, hired Balmat to accompany him on an attempt for the summit. He had personally done a good deal of reconnoitring on the lower slopes, and had a real and scientific interest in reaching the summit, much like De Saussure. Balmat was otherwise motivated: by thoughts of fame and fortune. He was rather a difficult character, and Paccard would probably not have chosen him were it not for his high-altitude bivouac (albeit one that came about through his habit of simply wandering away from parties he accompanied).

Following the route already known as the 'Ancien Passage', the two left on 7 August 1786, and after two bivouacs and considerable hardships, including a near miss on a large crevasse, summitted on 9 August, returning to the Montagne de la Cote hut by midnight. It was a bold and spirited venture into the unknown, which brought fame to Balmat in particular. Balmat led a delighted De Saussure to the summit in August 1787, and was honoured with an award by King Vittorio, and a statue in Chamonix. Paccard had no need for the reward, or for the glory, but after years of controversy and allegations that he was 'dragged up', fuelled by the boasts of Balmat, he eventually made his own vital role known in a document which he compelled Balmat to sign. It took almost 150 years before he, too, was properly acknowledged, as a result of the efforts of the 'Paccard Society', by a bust erected in 1932 in Chamonix.

The peak attracts thousands of climbers each year, spurred on by the term 'highest in Europe'. It is, in fact, the highest in Western Europe, with the

Top left Bill O'Connor in action in true traditional style on Arête des Cosmiques, Aiguille du Midi.
Centre left Joss Cleave on the Southeast Ridge of Mont Blanc, with Aiguille de la République in the distance.
Bottom left Spindrift in the Supercouloir, Mont Blanc du Tacul – one of the finest test pieces in the range.
Opposite A group of climbers moving through fresh snow at the head of the Vallée Blanche, Mont Blanc.

5633m (18,482ft) Caucasus peak, Elbrus, being the highest summit in greater Europe. Despite many of the routes being of little technical difficulty, the altitude, the fickle nature of the weather, and the presence of numerous, often hidden, crevasses on all of the routes leads to the loss of some hundreds of lives each season. It is estimated that some 7000 people have to date lost their lives on Mont Blanc itself, a disturbing proportion on the busy 'normal' routes. The notorious traverse of the stonefall-prone Grand Couloir of the Aiguille du Goûter on the Goûter-Bosses Ridge ascent (the *voie normale*) accounts for a number each year, despite the presence of a fixed rope. The guides refer to this section as the 'Russian Roulette' traverse, with difficult-to-avoid stones whistling down frequently and unpredictably.

Many superb routes can be found on the large and complex Mont Blanc massif. The earliest explorers of the vast number of satellite peaks include Edward Whymper and his French guide, Michel Croz (of Matterhorn fame), and Alfred Mummery with his friend and guide Alex Burgener from Saas Fe. It is undoubtedly both the playground and the forcing ground of alpinism, with thousands of climbers repeating established climbs each year, while numerous new routes, necessarily of greater and greater difficulty, are still being forged.

THE CENTRAL PILLAR OF FRÊNEY

Looking up from the village of Courmayeur, the Italian side of Mont Blanc presents a far more formidable appearance than the northern French aspect. Of all these awe-inspiring peaks, the large and complex Brouillard and Frêney faces loom the most majestically. Under the highest visible point, the summit of Mont Blanc de Courmayeur, stand the immense granite pillars of the Frêney. These challenging routes start at over 3600m (11,800ft), higher than the summit of most other extreme Alpine faces. Difficult to access, with retreat under bad conditions being an extremely perilous challenge, these were eyed longingly, but not seriously attempted until a bold

Left Rébuffat Route, South Face, Aiguille du Midi, Mont Blanc range, is a vertical feast of granite.

thrust was finally made in war-torn Europe in 1940. The right-hand pillar (now known as the Gervasutti Pillar) was climbed by Giusto Gervasutti and Paulo Bollini in a determined, and for many years unrepeated, effort.

The real 'plum' route, however, was considered to be the Central Pillar of Frêney, with its imposing and seemingly impenetrable rock band. It was attempted on a number of occasions, but not completed until 1961, when three determined groups made their attempts. The first climb led to disaster, when four of seven top alpinists lost their lives trying to retreat from the 80m (262ft) cliff feature known as the 'Chandelle' (the candle) in a heavy storm. The party consisted of Antoine Vieille, Pierre Kohlmann, Robert Guillaume and Andrea Oggioni (all of whom died of exposure and exhaustion on the descent via the Rochers Gruber), as well as Walter Bonatti, Pierre Mazeaud and Roberto Gallieni, who only just managed to get out alive. The seven climbers from France and Italy, all regarded as the top in their field, had met at the tiny bivouac box on the Col de la Fourche on the night of 10 July 1961, and decided to join forces to solve 'the last great problem' of the time. All had been involved in previous attempts on the Pillar. They reached the 80m-high (260ft) cliff on 11 July, when a storm of epic proportions broke. For two days the men pressed, unsheltered and ice-shrouded, against the rock face. On the third day, in atrocious weather, they attempted a retreat via long, difficult abseils on stiff, iced-up ropes in driving wind, rain, hail and snow. All made it to a crevasse bivouac on the Col de Peuterey on the night of 14 July. The four men died one by one of exhaustion and hypothermia while fighting their way through the tempest on the morning of 15 July, with their equally exhausted comrades frustratingly unable to assist them. One of the three survivors, Walter Bonatti, was the subject of much unwarranted criticism. His critics pointed out the similarity in the circumstances of another climb – he had been one of two left alive on a retreat from the Brenva Ridge in 1956, when his climbing partners, J Vincendon and F Henry,

Right Alpine climbing on the Gervasutti Pillar at the start to the Supercouloir, Mont Blanc.

died. These accusations stung Bonatti, who had been the subject of controversies over the years; he retreated from the climbing scene for a few years, returning to the public eye only in 1965 with his masterful solo winter ascent of a new direct route on the North Face of the Matterhorn.

A month after the Bonatti epic an Anglo-Polish group, consisting of Chris Bonington, Don Whillans, Ian Clough and Jan Dlugosz, made its way from the Col de la Fourche hut (3680m; 12,074ft) to the Col de Peuterey, then to the foot of the pillars via the Frêney Glacier – a seven-hour journey. The pillars are guarded by a complex bergschrund (*see* page 159), which always causes delays. By this stage the party was aware of another group headed in the same direction –

Frenchmen René Desmaison and Pierre Julien, and Italians Yves Pollet-Villard and Ignazio Piussi. National honour demanded that the largely British team 'get a move on' (in the words of Whillans), which they did. A bold traverse disposed of the bergschrund. They quickly dispatched the first few pitches of mixed climbing, and the first steepish rock step with three pitches of moderate Grade V.

Below, left to right Looking back along the Goûter Ridge on the way to the summit of Mont Blanc; a view south into Italy from the summit of Mont Blanc, with the Gran Paradiso in the background; climbers descend the heavily corniced Bosses Ridge, where the contrast between shadow and light is striking.

Opposite A magnificent view of Mont Blanc as seen from the Aiguille du Midi. The *voie normale* follows the skyline on the right-hand side.

Right A climber on the edge of the Arête des Cosmiques, Aiguille du Midi. This moderate route is particularly spectacular in winter.

A few traverse pitches, a steep snow ramp, and then a Grade VI chimney-crack led back to the foot of the Chandelle. This vertical and even over-hanging section had proven to be the 'stopper' crux on previous attempts. After a long struggle Whillans, one of the best climbers in the world, took a huge 20m (70ft) fall, and it was left to Bonington to complete the remaining 60m (200ft) section at Grade VI/A2. A still shaken but determined Whillans followed; then, in gathering darkness, Clough and Dlugosz prussiked up (*see* page 159). The party found a small, uncomfortable bivouac ledge in a looming storm, but luckily the weather held. The next day, after completing the rock section – a few broken slab pitches – they did an abseil and some 45-degree mixed ground to the Brouillard Ridge and hence over easy ground to the summit. The French-Italian party reached the summit hot on their heels a few hours later.

There were some scathing comments in climbing journals when, following their claims to the second ascent, it was learned that they had overcome the tortuous crux section by prussiking up a rope which Clough had left in place. No-one in their party had actually led the difficult section which had stopped so many parties in the past – somewhat of a breach in ethics.

The Central Pillar is still highly regarded, and its difficult Chandelle section continues to lure climbers. In 1991 Jean-Christian Lafaille opened (solo) the committing L'Ecume des Jours (ED, 6c, A3), a slightly more direct line than the 1961 classic, but parallelling it on the Chandelle.

Sadly, the Central Pillar of Frêney has seen quite a number of tragedies with the same results as that of Bonatti and his party. This great 'extreme' classic route is not really the place for the average alpinist, but rather for the specialist who has the necessary skills and judgement to deal with the vagaries of Alpine weather.

The Matterhorn

The Chocolate-box Peak

Its unique chocolate-box beauty and dramatic history places the Matterhorn firmly alongside Everest in the 'world's best-known peaks' category. It is a spectacular mountain, a soaring pyramid that has four distinct faces and four clean-cut ridges, giving it both aesthetic splendour and mountaineering appeal.

In 1865 Edward Whymper, the famous British climber, was in Italy to make another attempt on the peak, having adopted it as 'his mountain'. He had made eight attempts over the previous four years, including a solo attempt on the Lion Ridge in 1862 which nearly ended in tragedy when he slipped and fell many metres.

Whymper once again booked César Carrel – a guide with whom he had made six previous attempts – to tackle the East Face and Ridge, but Carrel, it turned out, had secretly arranged to try the Italian Ridge with a group that included a wealthy Italian, Quintino Sella, in order to claim the peak for his native Italy. Whymper, furious at the deception, decided to go to Zermatt to try his own attack on the Hörnli Ridge. There he met young Lord Francis Douglas who, although only 18, was in his third Alpine season and had completed numerous first ascents. They engaged Peter Taugwalder and his son as guides, as well as Michel Croz, who had coincidentally arrived in Zermatt with his client, the Reverend Charles Hudson. The latter had a large number of guideless climbs to his credit, including the first ascent of the Bosses Ridge of Mont Blanc. Accompanying him was the 19-year-

MATTERHORN 4477m

—— *Italian Ridge 1911*
----- *Fürggen Ridge 1911*
- - - *Cresta de Amicis 1933*
— — *'Diretissima' 1983*

old Douglas Hadow, only in his first season, but with a number of Alpine ascents, including Mont Blanc, to his credit.

The group agreed to join forces, though Whymper was not entirely happy about Hadow's lack of rock-climbing expertise. At 05:30 on 13 July 1865, the group set off from Zermatt under clear skies. By noon they had pitched a tent at 3350m (11,000ft) on the East Face, just off the Hörnli Ridge. The ridge had proven easier than expected, and the group's spirits were high. They were determined to beat the Italian party.

The following day Hudson and Whymper took turns to lead up the great sweep of the East Face and Northeast Ridge. The party moved rapidly onwards, over loose rocks and patches of snow and ice, eventually overcoming the steepish last few hundred feet to the summit by moving onto the Northeast Face. From here they looked down in triumph on the Italian party, still struggling up near the shoulder of the Lion Ridge. Whymper's group knocked down some 'smallish' rocks, ostensibly to 'attract the Italians' attention' – which they doubtless did!

On the steepest section of the descent, directly above the great drop of the North Face, Hadow slipped. In the process he knocked Croz off his feet, and Douglas and Hudson in turn were also dragged down. The rope connecting the four to Taugwalder Senior broke, causing the quartet to plunge to their death down the steep East Face, watched helplessly by a horrified Whymper and the Taugwalder father and son.

Opposite The lovely Matterhorn in all its winter beauty. The North Face is clearly visible on the right.
Top right Climbing on the unremitting North Face, with the Pinnacles of Zmutt to the extreme right.
Bottom right Abseil retreat down the North Face by Niki Clough; the peaks of Mischabel rise beyond.

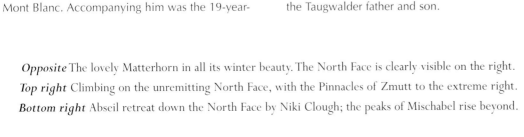

The subsequent tale of triumph and tragedy scandalized the climbing world. Blame was put alternatively onto Whymper, the Taugwalders, other members of the party, the rope, fate, and the gods. The 'Whymper saga' shows how the media can twist a mountaineering accident into a major public scandal. For years mountaineering suffered from the taint of the Matterhorn accident.

But the notoriety of the peak soon turned into fame. By the end of 1867 both the Hörnli and Lion ridges had huts, fixed ropes and ladders to aid in the ascent of guided parties.

The peak has had its fair share of tragedy – it is estimated that over 500 people have died here, mostly on the two easier routes. After a new snow-fall, the mountain changes its character suddenly, and inexperienced parties on the ridges can get into difficulties. Perhaps the saddest deaths were those of a young German couple who fell on the ascent – they were to have been married on the summit.

Above The Matterhorn summit – a small but often crowded area with a multitude of loose rocks.

Right A climber on the Hörnli Ridge, some 600m (1970ft) below the summit of the Matterhorn.

THE NORTH FACE

In the Alps, north faces are special – colder, steeper and harder than their southern opposites. The Matterhorn North Face was unsuccessfully attempted for nearly 50 years before a pair of Munich brothers, Franz and Toni Schmid, confounded pessimistic 'experts' by climbing to the summit in 34 nonstop hours on 31 July 1931. Their route up the great curving couloir in the middle of the steep face was more than equal to the hardest routes of the day.

In 1965 – the Centennial Jubilee of the Whymper ascent – celebrated alpinist Walter Bonatti put up a new *diretissima* on the North Face, ushering in a spectacular new dimension in alpinism by climbing solo under extreme conditions. A single slip, a single error, could have led to disaster during his four days' climbing in –25°C (–13°F) temperatures.

This was Bonatti's swan song – his 'romantic impulse'. At the age of 34, he abandoned cutting-edge alpinism. 'I was no longer pursuing the top of the mountain, I was using the mountain to measure myself. The mountain is the means, the man the end. The idea is to improve the man, not to reach the top of the mountain.' (Bonatti, as quoted in *Beyond Risk*.) Bonatti is a deep-thinking, philosophical mountaineer, whose influence on climbing has been without precedence.

The Eiger

The 'Mordwand' – Wall of Death

After Everest, the Eiger in west-central Switzerland is probably the best-known mountain in the world. There are many reasons for this fame, or notoriety, including a number of books and at least two major feature films which have highlighted the peak. For many years it repelled the world's leading climbers, and it has a chilling death toll.

For the climber, too, it has an almost macabre appeal. The great wall of snow, ice and dark black rock looms over the valley at Grindelwald. So vast and steep is the face that it appears completely overhanging.

The Eiger is accessible to observers – from the hotels at Kleine Scheidegg every move of the climbers can be watched through high-powered telescopes, rivalling 'live action' television coverage of a boxing tournament for blow-by-blow excitement! The incredible Eiger railway, completed in 1912, with its carved tunnels rising for thousands of metres through the heart of the mountain up to the Jungfraujoch, adds to the mystique and accessibility of the huge rock wall through which it cuts.

Some eight full routes (excluding variations) now pierce the triangular rampart of this mountain, and few have originated without drama and sacrifice. The Eiger North Face, on the edge of the range, catches bad weather as it approaches rapidly and without warning from the north and west. So high is it that it has its own weather patterns – frequently the bowl of the wall is shrouded in mist, battered by storm, rain and snow, while the sun shines deceptively on the lovely valley below. The great danger is from falling stones and ice. Every ledge is piled with loose scree, which freezes at night and is held captive, only to plunge down on unfortunate climbers as the ice loosens its grip during the day. Speed is of the essence, and many less experienced parties fall short in this vital element.

The first serious attempt on the Nordwand (North Wall) of the Eiger was made in 1935. Europe was caught up in financial uncertainties after the Depression years, and the tides of nationalism and war were lapping at the nations' boundaries. For the young climbers eyeing the greatest prize of the climbing world there were, however, no political considerations – merely the thrill of being the first to succeed on this bastion.

In early August, Max Sedlmayer and Karl Mehringer, both in their early 20s, set out with provisions for six days. They made good time at first, and the watchers were impressed with their skill. Then the great ice fields seemed to slow them down, and it took two full days to cross the first and second ice fields. The weather closed in, and watchers lost sight of the pair. They were not seen again until 19 September, when the German air ace, Ernst Udet, flew close enough to the wall for the bodies to be spotted at what was thereafter called the 'Death Bivouac' on the upper rim of the third ice field. The Nordwand had claimed its first victims.

EIGER 3970m

———— Heckmair Route 1938
- - - - Southwest Flank & West Ridge 1858
— — Lauper Route 1964
· · · · · Harlin Direct Route 1966

Top left James Kigambi stands triumphantly on the summit after the first Kenyan ascent of Mittellegi Ridge.

Centre left A deceptively benign-looking Eiger looms over Kleine Scheidegg, the North Face half in shadow.

Bottom left Haston and Bonington on a winter recce below the First Band cliffs on the Eiger North Face.

Opposite The North Face of the Eiger in a rare dry summer – this is as steep and serious as it gets.

THE EIGER DIRECT

Many climbers have used the term 'the last great alpine problem'; if the term should be attributed to any route, most feel that this route should be the Eiger Direct.

The concept of the diretissima represents the quintessence of climbing. There is no other face or line which can match this Eiger diretissima — the Eiger is justifiably called the 'Largest Wall in the Alps'. The American guide John Harlin, then the director of the International School of Mountaineering in Leysin, Switzerland, conceived the idea of doing the Eiger Direct in the winter of 1966 with Britain's Dougal Haston, reducing stonefall risk at the expense of freezing conditions. Normal Alpine tactics did not, however, suffice, and the American–British team eventually joined forces with a German party led by Jörg Lehne, using virtual Himalayan siege tactics — ferrying loads, digging snowholes, jumaring (see page 159) up the ropes. The climb took from 23 February to 25 March.

It was this jumaring that caused the tragedy of the climb, when the rope on which John Harlin was ascending to the level of the Spider frayed right through and he plunged to his death, with the party only a few days from success. The climbers decided to finish the route despite the accident, and named the route the Harlin Route in John's honour and memory.

LAYTON KOR BELAYING HARLIN NEAR THE TOP OF THE SECOND ICE FIELD, EIGER DIRECT, 1966.

Above John Harlin huddles in a snow cave on the Eiger North Face, Eiger Direct, 1966.

Right Grindelwald and the Eiger in their pristine winter mantle of snow.

Below The victorious although saddened team of climbers after the first ascent of the Eiger by the direct route in 1966.

The next year saw the Toni Kurz tragedy. On 18 July, two Austrians, Edi Rainer and Willy Angerer, and two Bavarians, Anderl Hinterstoisser and Toni Kurz, set out to follow the path set by the 1935 pair. They took a slightly different route, with Anderl crossing the now-famous Hinterstoisser Traverse, to link the Rote Fluh to the first ice field. He used the Dülfer tension technique – a rope tensioned from slightly above and to the side is used to assist the lead climber to lay a 'traverse rope'. The rest followed easily, but made the fatal mistake of pulling the traverse rope out of its pitons. They took three days to reach the end of the third ice field, but Angerer was struck by a stone and they had to retreat. They failed to cross the Hinterstoisser Traverse, by now iced up, and had to try to descend directly from the first ice field to the Eigerwand station. Anderl came off the face and pulled the rest with him into the valley below. Kurz was left suspended on the broken rope, the only one alive, just 30m (100ft) above the station window. His cries could be heard clearly. Watched by horrified hotel guests below, desperate attempts were made to save him, but the rescuers were unable to climb up the face

in the storm. With great effort the frozen figure at last managed to join the pieces of his frayed rope, and lower it to the rescuers, who had gone out onto the face despite the edict of the chief guide that 'no more rescues must be attempted by local guides on this murderous Nordwand'. Kurz hauled up two joined ropes, and abseiled to within feet of his rescuers before his carabiner jammed on a knot, leaving him hanging in space just below the edge of the overhang above the gallery window. With a cry of: 'It is over!' he died from exhaustion and exposure in full view of his weeping rescuers.

The year 1937 saw six unsuccessful attempts, one death and two rescues. The press berated the 'idiots on the mountain of death' and the North Face was nicknamed the 'Mordwand' ('wall of death').

In June 1938 Italians Bartalo Sandri and Mario Menti died in a storm just above Difficult Crack. The climbers camping in the valley were shaken, but not discouraged. A long, nerve-wracking wait ensued. By mid-July the face was in slightly better condition, and Austrian climbers Fritz Kasparek and Heinrich Harrer started up the wall. The First Pillar and Shattered Pillar went rapidly, as did Difficult Crack and Rote Fluh; they bivouacked on top of the latter. Then the Hinterstoisser Traverse was crossed, two years to the day after the death of the Hinterstoisser party – this time, the traverse rope was left in case of retreat.

All went well, even the Ice Hose with its torrent of cold water. Then came the second ice field. The true nature of the Eiger was encountered there, as stones and ice hurtled down unpredictably. It took two hours to cross the dangerous 500m (1500ft) of 'wet cathedral roof'. Looking back, they saw two well-equipped climbers, Anderl Heckmair and

Ludwig Vörg from Munich, virtually running across the ice field! They were using the new 12-point crampons, with front points, allowing far more efficient climbing, and had covered the route in only one day. Harrer had no crampons, only nailed boots, which cost the pair a fair amount of time. The four joined forces to climb as one party, albeit in two roped pairs. The speed and modern equipment of the German pair aided Harrer and Kasparek, who might otherwise have been trapped in the brewing storm.

The group climbed up the Flatiron, past Death Bivouac, diagonally down the steep third ice field to the foot of the Ramp. Kasparek took a 20m (60ft) tumble off the Ramp, but ploughed back on immediately, determined to complete the pitch. By this stage, the telescopes in the valley were fetching a good price, with watchers booking time hours in advance, whether they could see or not, and a number of fights broke out. The press commented that '... this time there were more and greater injuries among the observers in the valley than the climbers on the great Nordwand'.

Night-time forced a precarious bivouac, with Kasparek and Harrer suspended from one tiny piton, fixed only 1cm (½in) deep in a crack!

Early the following morning, they continued to make their way up the icy Ramp gully. Heckmair fell off, but then went on to surmount the ice bulge in superb style. He led on, not removing his crampons to save time, over 30m (100ft) of rock – a bold and innovative action in those days, though fairly common now.

A violent thunderstorm preceded the Traverse of the Gods, that delicate traverse on friable rock. Then came the White Spider, with its fearsome gully-legs, catching ice, snow, sleet and stones and channelling these down on the puny figures scrabbling to cross it. It was here that an avalanche nearly tore all four climbers from the face – only a small piton and a dug-in ice axe saved the day. Kasparek hurt his hand badly, but at least all survived. Now only 300m (1000ft) from the summit, they finally joined up as a rope of four.

The weather threw everything at them – snow, hail, and rain. They managed a marginal bivouac on a narrow ledge. Morning dawned gloomy, with a gale and constant avalanches. It was move or freeze, so they committed themselves to a 'do-or-die' attempt. This was Heckmair's day of glory – he was unstoppable, and led brilliantly for the entire day: up the icy exit cracks, with many slips and falls, blindly through the snow onto the curving summit ice field. At 15:30, he just managed to stop himself walking right over the South Face. After 85 hours (61 for Vörg and Heckmair) the North Face had been overcome!

The German–Austrian quartet was honoured by Hitler, which led to controversy and criticism, some of which is still heard today. Among climbers, ascending that face was sufficient. However, what politicians made of such an achievement was of no real consequence to the four. 'We climbed the Eiger's North Face because it proved an irresistible challenge to our courage and our love of adventure, not for medals or rewards.' (Heinrich Harrer, *The White Spider*.)

Ludwig Vörg was killed on the Russian front in 1941; Kasparek died when the summit cornice gave way on Salcantay in Peru in 1954. Heckmair and Harrer are still alive; the latter is now embroiled in bitter and, in truth, unnecessary controversy over his supposed German nationalist role after the Eiger success.

The Eiger now boasts a number of routes on the North Face. It has been soloed in a few hours, ascended in winter, and has seen many rescues. It is not and never will be 'an easy day for a lady', to quote (or misquote) Mummery. Brian Nally, after being rescued in 1962 following the death of his companion, said: 'It's a pig of a face – but somehow it's the final test of how good you are in the Alps … I know that it's better than us.'

On the first three solo attempts, the climbers died; on the fourth, Walter Bonatti retreated, saying : 'No mountain is worth as much as one's life.' Michel Darbellay, a Swiss guide, succceeded in soloing it over two days in August 1963.

It will doubtless see more routes established on its sombre, overhanging cliffs. It is still regarded as a test piece, and its conquest is desired by all aspirant 'alpine hard men'. It is not for the unwary, the novice, or the faint of heart. It is, after all, still the Eiger Mordwand, with its well-deserved reputation.

Left The famous Mittellegi Ridge is essentially a rock climb. The elegant Mönch is on the left.

The Petit Dru

Great Things Come in Small Packages

Seen from the little Alpine town of Montenvers in France, the Aiguille du Dru appears in the form of a giant, triangular rock obelisk, one of the most striking features on the Mont Blanc range. It has two summits: the Grand Dru, at 3754m (12,317ft), and its 20m (60ft) shorter little sister, the Petit Dru. The modern climbs for which the mountain is most famous all lie on the steep Petit Dru.

The Grand Dru was first climbed in 1878 by three British climbers – Clinton Dent, Horace Walker and John Maund – together with Alex Burgener from Switzerland, after Dent's 'insane obsession with the peak' had led him to attempt it no less than 19 times. It was one of the most sought-after peaks and no one sought it more assiduously than Dent, a Harley Street surgeon, with his guide, Burgener. Dent later became the president of the Alpine Club.

PETIT DRU 3733m

—— *Bonatti Route 1955*

The first ascents of the major faces of the Petit Dru read like the Who's Who of Alpine climbing for each successive era. The famous guides Jean Charlet-Stratton, P Payot and F Folliguet first ascended in 1879; the first Petit–Grand traverse was by E Giraud, Joseph Ravanel and E Comte; the North Face by the great French climber Pierre Allain, with R Leininger, in 1935; the West Face by Guido Magnone, M Laine, A Dagory and L Berardini in 1952; and the two 'American Direct' routes on the West Face by Guy Hemmings and Royal Robbins in 1962, and John Harlin and Robbins in 1965.

THE BONATTI PILLAR

Probably the most famous route in the Dru's was the solo ascent of the Southwest Pillar in August 1955 by the 24-year-old Walter Bonatti, who had just returned, discouraged, from the successful Italian K2 expedition, where he had sacrificed his own chance of going for the summit by helping Lacedelli and Compagnoni. A communication problem between Bonatti and Lacedelli had led to unwarranted criticism of Bonatti by the expedition leader, and he was hurt and resentful. It was in this frame of mind that he sought a 'great challenge', and the solo of the Southwest Pillar of the Petit Dru proved to be just that.

Solo climbing is perhaps the ultimate expression of the sport, as the climber is thrown totally onto his own resources. It was this freedom that Bonatti sought and found on the Petit Dru. He was determined to tackle the almost unthinkable – a solo attempt on a new route which everyone predicted would be the most challenging route ever done in the Alps.

Bonatti set out at about 02:00 on 15 August, his huge kitbag heavily laden. The pillar begins some 400m (1300ft) up the dangerous couloir leading to the base of the multispiked Flammes de Pierre, then continues on superb granite. The climb is characterized by its sustained nature, with most pitches being Grade V or above, and its famous series of clean-cut dièdres (*see* page 159) and corner cracks.

Opposite The West Face was first completed in 1952, and in 1955 Bonatti climbed the Southwest Pillar.
Top right This view from the Wall of the Petit Dru to Mont Blanc shows the steepness of the climb.
Bottom right The Bonatti Pillar, with the famous '40m layback' in the centre, the bottom third.

At 08:00 an exhausted Bonatti dragged his 36kg (80 lb) load up the deep gully towards the foot of the climb. Eventually he gave up on this approach, abandoned a lot of food and gear, and descended. The next day, with a few friends, he ferried the equipment around to the Charpoua

Top A climber on Bonatti Pillar – a superb granite structure with a vast nothingness below.

Right The 14km (9-mile) Mer de Glace winds picturesquely between the peaks of the Western Mont Blanc group.

Opposite A splendid view of the Petit Dru with its veil of clouds, as seen from the east, with the Bonatti Pillar in profile on the right.

Hut on the other side of the Flammes Ridge. On 17 August he climbed solo up to the ridge and abseiled for about 250m (800ft) to the base of the pillar. While driving in a piton, he smashed off the tip of his third finger. Worse was to come – his fuel had leaked out, contaminating most of

the food and also denying him the hot drinks he would need. He climbed the pillar largely as a 'roped solo' – he would tie the rope to the sack, anchor it to the rock, then lead out, clipping the trailing rope into subsidiary pitons he placed as he ascended. From the end of this pitch, he would then abseil down, clearing pitons, then jumar up and haul up the sack.

For six days Bonatti kept at it. On the fifth day he had to surmount the huge overhang barring the way up. He was dehydrated and hungry. Up on the overhanging wall, the thin crack he was aid-climbing pinched out. He spied another crack line 20m (65ft) away, and attempted to pendulum to it, ending up on a small platform 12m (40ft) short of the crack. There was no way up and no possibility of abseil retreat. As a final desperate measure, he lassoed a small hand-

shaped prong above him, and used this tenuous point to complete his pendulum. 'A last unnerving delay, a last inner prayer for safety. I closed my eyes for a second, held my breath and let myself slip into space, holding the rope with both hands.' (Bonatti, *On the Heights*.) The plan worked, and he was able to climb on. He recalls having long conversations with his rucksack, and with in-visible companions who hovered around him. Fatigue, dehydration and lack of food were keeping him in a state of semi-delirium. At 16:30 on 22 August, Bonatti, his hands raw and bleeding, reached the summit, laying to rest the demons of K2 which had plagued him for so long.

The Petit Dru has seen many sensational ascents, including that of Christopher Profit, who did a daring free (unroped) solo of the American Direct route in front of television cameras, with the sound recording of his laboured breathing and mutterings creating some of the most spine-tingling footage of climbing ever made.

In 1990 Catherine Destivelle took only four hours to complete a solo of the Bonatti route. She disliked the comparisons the media made

between her time and Bonatti's (mainly because he was her major inspiration), so in 1991 she opened her own new route, solo, right next to Bonatti's. This took her a whole 11 days of climbing, much of it on aid and also in snowy conditions. She hauled a hefty 64kg (142 lb) of food and equipment all the way up the face. This was the first time a solo female climber had opened a major difficult route on an Alpine peak – although Destivelle is quite adamant that she did not do it to make any form of feminist statement whatsoever. 'In the end, climbing comes before all else … and I take my renewed pleasure in doing it for myself alone. For the moment, things are going fine, and I live passionately; there is great pleasure in this and it takes care of everything else.' (Catherine Destivelle, *Ballerina of the Rocks*.)

Mount Cook

Aorangi – the Mont Blanc of the South

Although in the late 19th century New Zealand was many long, slow sea miles away from the European Alps, the feats of Alpine climbers had nonetheless reached the ears of New Zealanders. In 1882 the Reverend William Spottiswood Green, a 35-year-old Irish clergyman, made the first of many attempts on Mount Cook (known to the Maori as Aorangi) in the Southern Alps on South Island. He was accompanied by Emil Boss and Ulrich Kaufmann from Grindelwald. They climbed the great Tasman Glacier, and then the Hooker, setting up four camps on the glacier itself – narrowly spaced by modern standards, but their equipment, including a gun and cartridges, and 12kg (25 lb) of duck and mutton, weighed several hundred pounds. The slopes were dangerous, the rock being a loose conglomerate of pebbles and sand called 'grey-wacke'.

The mountains of New Zealand, often referred to as 'Southern Switzerland', are lower than the European Alps, but their proximity to the sea gives them a lower permanent snowline – some 600m (2000ft) lower, at about 2100m (7000ft). Measured from the snowline, Mount Cook is thus the 'same height' as Mont Blanc. The weather is generally poorer than in the Alps, with heavy precipitation and the high winds of the 'Roaring Forties' creating impressive ice formations. The first attempt via the Ball Glacier and South Ridge proved abortive, an unstable snow ridge turning the Green party back at just 2285m (7500ft). They tried to get higher up the treacherous Ball Glacier, and ended up on a minefield of

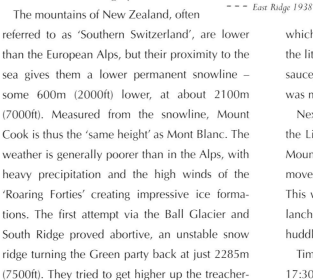

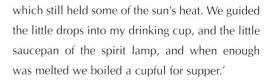

----- North Ridge 1894
— — Zurbriggen's Ridge 1895
——— Linda Glacier 1912
- - - East Ridge 1938

ice pinnacles and blocks. They overcame these obstacles by extensive step-cutting, only to reach a huge cliff beset with avalanches. They retreated in frustration at 2438m (8000ft). Some days later they reached a narrow ridge on the north of the Hochstetter Glacier, and, heavily laden with the standard equipment of the day (an oil cloth sheet, a sleeping bag, an opossum rug, food for three days, two 20m, or 60ft, ropes and heavy cameras), they set off up the face to their first bivouac. From Green's account in *The Trials of Mount Cook*: 'While Kaufmann scraped a smooth place under the rock, arranging the stones with their sharpest angles downwards and making a nice bed for us of material somewhat like road metal, Boss and I melted snow by spreading it out on boulders which still held some of the sun's heat. We guided the little drops into my drinking cup, and the little saucepan of the spirit lamp, and when enough was melted we boiled a cupful for supper.'

Next day they reached the Great Plateau and the Linda Glacier, which links Mount Cook with Mount Tasman. Despite threatening weather, they moved onto a couloir parallel to the North Ridge. This was nearly the end of them, as a huge avalanche hurtled down, passing over them as they huddled behind small rognons (stone blocks).

Time was running against them and finally, at 17:30, with no sleeping bags or other supplies, a large bergschrund made them decide to turn back.

Opposite The very steep Linda Face of Mount Cook offers the modern climber many interesting challenges.
Top left The Summit Ridge often becomes heavily corniced when sudden violent storms strike the peak.
Centre left The 'Southern Alps' offer ice-climbers outstanding solid ice, on a par with the best in Europe.
Bottom left A climber on steep ice, Mount Cook. Demanding routes are being pioneered in the range.

Records would later prove that they were only 60m (200ft) below the summit! They spent the night standing in the pelting rain on a ledge 50cm (2ft) wide, clinging to the rock face, terrified lest they fall asleep and plunge into the abyss below.

Arthur Harper, who founded the New Zealand Alpine Club, made the next five attempts. With him was George Mannering. They, too, failed 40m (150ft) short of the summit on their last attempt.

Finally came the 'Christmas Party'. Three New Zealanders – George Graham, Jack Clark and Thomas Fyfe, a professional guide – went via the Hooker Glacier and North Ridge, an exacting route with loose rock and hanging ice. Despite the dangers of the route, they had a trouble-free ascent, reaching the summit on 25 December 1884. All descended safely and in good spirits to a belated but jubilant Christmas celebration. Lest one makes too light of their efforts because of the apparent

ease of ascent, it is worth noting that, despite the efforts of many good climbers, this route did not see a repeat ascent for 61 years!

The next ascent was equally amazing for its time. Edward Fitzgerald, the great dilettante climber, arrived with Matthias Zurbriggen, his companion and a professional guide, within a week of the first ascent. Fitzgerald was so disappointed at not 'bagging the peak' that he didn't even attempt to climb it, but Zurbriggen did – solo, via the Linda Glacier and the buttress that had turned William Spottiswood Green back. Fitzgerald and Zurbriggen went on to claim the first ascent of Mount Tasman (3497m; 11,475ft) in 1894.

Mount Cook still has some excellent routes. To appreciate its severe nature, it was, after all, the training ground of Sir Edmund Hillary. In 1991 the top 15m (50ft) of the mountain cascaded down the East Face, taking a few thousand tons of

ice and boulders with it. The debris travelled 5km (3 miles) across the Tasman Glacier and 300m (1000ft) up the other side. Mount Cook was left in peace by climbers for a while after that!

The mountains of New Zealand offer excellent ice and snow climbing, as well as rock and mixed faces in true Alpine tradition. Although all the peaks and most of the obvious lines have already been climbed, there is still scope for hard variation routes and winter ascents.

Opposite The Summit Ridge of Mount Cook, with some tricky broken ground yet to be covered en route to the summit.

Above A solo climber nears the top of the East Ridge at sunrise. The changeable wind direction has created a fine snow arête.

THE BIG WALLS

THE BIG WALLS

EL CAPITAN • CERRO TORRE • POLAR SUN SPIRE

How big is 'big'? And how do 'big walls' differ from big alpine walls? The answer is a matter of degree – many rock climbs verge on 'big wall' status, and many alpine routes have big walls which need to be overcome. The definition arises from a historical viewpoint; the big wall classification came about largely in the Yosemite Valley in the USA, and referred originally to the long routes on the walls of the valley, routes initially overcome with the aid of pitons, bolts and 'mechanized' climbing. These ascents lasted days or even weeks, with the climbers bivouacking on the wall, and hauling their gear up behind them.

The description later included all huge expanses of rock that were not strictly alpine – that is, they had a lower altitude than the European Alps and did not necessarily have a snow and ice approach or component. Many climbs that were multi-day affairs are now done in a few hours (some of the speed records in Yosemite are incredible – for example, four hours up routes that took weeks to open). Perhaps the best qualification for a big wall is that it should originally not have succumbed to climbers without a few days' worth of effort! The selection here ranges from the historical Yosemite routes in California to the newly opened Great and Secret Show at Sam Ford Fjord on Baffin Island, north of Canada and just south of the Arctic circle.

The greatest concentrations of big walls are to be found in North America – such as the 3000+m (10,000+ft) Moose's Tooth in Alaska and the Lotus Flower Tower in the Cirque of the Unclimbables – and in Patagonia, with the Paine group.

Paine is seen as one of the most severe climbing areas of the world, with high winds and extreme cold the order of the day. Whereas blue skies normally herald good climbing, they can be a curse in Patagonia. Antoine de Saint Exupery, in *Wind, Sand and Stars*, spoke of 'the blue sky, that glittered like a newly honed knife. The purity of the sky upset me – give me a good, black storm, where the enemy is clearly visible.' So climbers find it – an area where blue skies might suddenly spew forth frozen, express-train winds.

Paine Grande fought off six attempts before an Italian expedition with Walter Bonatti ascended it in 1957. Paine's Central Tower was only ascended in 1963, by a strong seven-man British team with Chris Bonington, Ian Clough and Don Whillans, in an interesting race with an Italian team. The Brits had pioneered only a fraction of the route when the Italian team arrived with the same goal in mind. Both parties attacked the face, but made little progress in the high winds. Early one morning the Brits awoke to total calm and quietly left their tents. It was only much later that the Italians saw their rivals high on the face. They rushed to the British ropes and started using them to ascend. The British rearguard pulled the higher ropes up away from the Italians, who climbed on using their own gear but following the British line. Bonington and Whillans made the summit at 19:30. Next morning they abseiled past the disappointed Italians, who only gained the summit at 17:00 that day.

In 1974 a South African team ascended first the Sword and then the East Face of Central Tower – the latter taking two months due to bad weather. In 1990 a German team including Wolfgang Güllich put up Riders in the Storm, a desperately hard route adjacent to the South African route.

It might seem a long step from the warmth of Yosemite to the cold of Patagonia, but the essence remains the same – to subdue immense expanses of vertical rock by any reasonable means.

EL CAPITAN

Location: Yosemite Valley, California, USA
Summit height: 2305m (7562ft)
Face height: 915m (3000ft)
First ascent: East Face – Al Steck, William Sim, Willi Unsoeld, Bill Lang (all USA), 1953; The Nose – Warren Harding, Wayne Merry, George Whitmore (all USA), 1958

CERRO TORRE

Location: Fitzroy Group, Patagonia, South America
Summit height: 3133m (10,280ft)
Face height: 1280m (4200ft)
First ascent: Peak, via North Face – Cesare Maestri (Italy) and Toni Egger (Austria), 1959 (disputed); Southeast Ridge and Pillar (Compressor route) – Maestri, 1971 (disputed); West Face – Casimiro Ferrari (Italy) and the 'Lecco Spiders', 1974

POLAR SUN SPIRE

Location: Sam Ford Fjord, Baffin Island
Summit height: 1340m (4400ft)
Face height: 1340m (4400ft)
First ascent: The Great and Secret Show – Warren Hollinger, Mark Synott, Jeff Chapman (all USA), 1996

Previous pages A view across the Yosemite Valley from a portaledge bivouac on El Capitan's lower reaches.
Opposite Fitzroy in Patagonia and its ramparts of steep rock, with Laguna de los Tres in the foreground.
Top right Bat Tent portaledges dangle precariously in space at Camp III on Trango Towers in Pakistan.

El Capitan

The Great North American Dream

It was the 1960s, the great 'hippie' era, and conservative-minded tourists to the Yosemite Valley in the Sierra Nevadas of California were both astonished and disgusted to see long-haired, colourfully garbed, beer-swilling (and sometimes even pot-smoking) figures walking along with bright ropes and clanking hardware. Yosemite became one of the favoured 'dropout zones' and a good number of fine young Americans came into climbing in this way.

Not all of the climbers were dropouts. Many were dedicated mountaineers, who held down jobs, or were studying, or had served their time in the military and were now getting down to their first love – climbing.

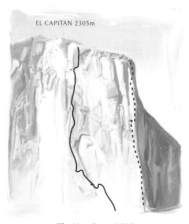

EL CAPITAN 2305m

---- *The Nose Route 1958*
—— *The Salathé Wall Route 1961*

Among the 'regulars' in the valley were those who were making climbing history, and creating a new type of climbing which would make its influence felt throughout the world. These were the pioneers of Big Wall Aid Climbing, an art that was developed on the massive granite walls of Yosemite.

In the late 1940s climbers such as Al Steck and Bob Swift put up the first really long route, the 360m (1200ft) Yosemite Point Buttress route. In 1950, Steck and John Salathé soon put up their next 'biggie' – the Salathé-Steck route on the North Face of the Sentinel, which many still consider to be one of the best climbs in the valley. Graded 5.9/A3, it was a superb achievement that took them all of four and a half hard-climbing days. Bivouacking on massive rock faces was still

unheard of, and their uncomfortable night-time perches set new standards of commitment for the generations to follow. Salathé had also made some very special pieces of gear for coping with the renowned Yosemite cracks – hard, specially shaped tungsten steel pitons, which bit into the rock, the wide range of sizes allowing previously unusable cracks to be climbed.

Dominating the valley are two major features – the great truncated expanse of the aptly named Half Dome, and the huge bulk of El Capitan ('El Cap'). Half Dome was the first to be scaled by a team that consisted of Royal Robbins with Jerry Gallwas, Don Wilson and Warren Harding on an abortive attempt in 1955 and, on the second, successful attempt in 1957, Robbins with Gallwas and Mike Sherrick. The Northwest Face route is 610m (2000ft) of completely sheer rock, and was the first Grade VI in America. The free-climbed pitches were long, serious, energy-draining layback cracks, or desperate friction slabs that demanded absolute concentration. Protection was vital – a fall would lead to a plunge of scores of metres, on ropes that might not hold. New protection and aid climbing techniques were literally being forged – Robbins' team, too, had made some special hard steel pitons, and had also placed 20 hand-drilled bolts to get them over the blank sections of rock. The special type of hard aid moves for which Yosemite was to become famous had begun.

Opposite The Southwest Face of El Capitan over the Merced River, with the Nose on the right-hand skyline.
Top left Paul Piana starting the last pitch of the headwall on the Salathé (Southwest Face) route, El Capitan.
Centre left Higher up on the same pitch, the vertical cracks offer little by way of handholds or protection.
Bottom left Todd Skinner leading the 5.11 pitch off El Capitan Spire on the Salathé route, Yosemite Valley.

THE NOSE ROUTE

The Nose route on El Capitan yet remained unclimbed. Warren Harding set his sights on it and, while Robbins was called away to do military service, sieged it over a period of 18 months. In a total of 47 days of climbing, abseiling down and then jumaring up to the previous high point, the Nose route was finally completed by Harding. Part of the success lay in the famous Salathé pitons, and part in the 'super protection of the day' – Harding had cut old stove legs to create large metal wedges, or bongs, for the wider cracks (primitive precursors of the huge range of wedges, bongs, pitons and camming devices available to today's climber). Harding had also used 125 hand-drilled bolt placements to conquer the Nose, a feat which caused severe controversy even then, and one which would not be permitted in today's Yosemite bolt-free (or rather, bolt-minimized) ethics. Nonetheless it was, for its time, an outstanding achievement, a true pioneering effort. The Great Roof pitch of the Nose, which plunges out into space, is still approached with awe and respect. The Nose was first climbed in a single day by Americans J Bridwell, J Long and B Westbay in 1975, and it was first free climbed in a day by the amazing Lynn Hill (also USA) in 1994.

Today the Nose route is one of the most popular climbs on El Capitan, and parties queue to attempt it. The average party completes the route in three to five days, with free climbing replacing a good deal of the earlier aid sections. Peter Croft and Hans Florine recently climbed the whole route in four hours and 22 minutes – a record that will take some beating. Speed climbing of Yosemite routes is rapidly becoming the most popular challenge for the current generation of climbers.

Left Spot the climbers – these three climbers are dwarfed by the overwhelming face of El Capitan, Yosemite National Park, giving some idea of the scale of the climbs.

Opposite A climber on the Nose of El Capitan, an endless sea of granite. The varied nature of modern Yosemite climbing can easily be seen here in the varied protection: there are pegs, nuts, 'Friends' and the odd fixed bolt.

THE SALATHÉ ROUTE

The Nose route was by no means the end of El Cap. The route which most climbers now regard as the most elegant and exciting was opened a year after the Nose. This was the Salathé route, named in honour of John Salathé, the great Yosemite pioneer. Royal Robbins, Tom Frost and Chuck Pratt threw themselves at the direct centre of the Southwest Face of El Capitan, a route that overhangs many metres, and one that at the time contained the hardest free rock and aid climbing yet done. Over a period of three weeks the trio pushed onwards and upwards. The first hundred or so metres went 'free', up to Heart Ledges. The team abseiled down to sleep and re-supply every night, and continued to do so for another 215m (700ft), until the huge overhanging upper headwall forced them to climb continuously with bivouacs. The haul sacks, now a regular feature of Yosemite big wall climbs, had to be dragged up behind the climbers. Retreat from the climb became impossible, as there was no way to get back onto the rock, so upwards was the only alternative. An injury at that time would have been

Above Half Dome seen from the valley floor.

Below Greg Lacey hand-jamming at Cookie, one of the pleasant 'short' climbs in the Yosemite Valley.

more than serious – a rescue could not be mounted from above, and it was not possible to swing back in under the overhangs on abseil. They were aware of this, and the climb became increasingly tense as cracks pinched out, leading them to do massive, body-jarring pendulums to adjoining crack systems, only to have the same thing happen thirty or so metres higher. After nine full days on the rock, the elated group finally reached the summit.

Modern training, techniques and equipment, coupled with intensive 'beta' (preknowledge of the route), have led to once-epic routes becoming quite commonplace. A current trend is to 'race' up routes, and both the Nose and the Salathé routes have been done in matters of hours; the Salathé has been both soloed and free-climbed.

Paul Piana who, with Todd Skinner, did the first free ascent of the Salathé, described the final section: 'This headwall must be the grandest in the Universe – an exquisite, inspiring crack system splitting the 100-degree sweep of golden wall at the top of El Capitan. The essence of the Salathé is distilled in this one fissure.' (Paul Piana, *The Free Salathé*.)

The pair rehearsed the 35-pitch route extensively, often on abseil, and they gained intimate knowledge of each difficult move over the space of a month. Only then did they feel ready for a bottom-to-top climb without pulling, standing or resting on any protection – a true 'free climb'.

'The hand jams were so bad that Todd had to visually monitor his hand during each move. So flaring were they that it was impossible to down-climb and the slightest error, even a change in blood pressure in his hand, would see the Salathé flick him off and send him screaming far below the roof … spinning thousands of feet off of the ground.' (Ibid) The climb was unrelenting, sustained, and most pitches went at grades from 5.11 to 5.13 – in the top order of difficulty. Eventually they emerged from the final pitch, victorious.

However, the epic was by no means over. While abseiling down to retrieve their gear, a huge, previously solid block to which some belay points were attached, slid over the edge, taking both the climbers with it. By some miracle, they found themselves injured but alive, hanging

Above Brian Gross below Great Roof, Nose Route.

Below Dave Austen on Misty Beethoven, Yosemite. Climbs tend to follow the natural crack lines.

from half-cut ropes – Skinner supported only by a mangled jumar, which had prevented his sole rope from being cut. They hauled themselves back over the edge, and made their shaky way down to base camp. 'We had dreamed, we had trained, and we had struggled. Even though the climb ended in a nightmare, we had triumphed. The ecstasy we feel at achieving our dream will live inside us forever.' (Ibid)

In September 1997, 28-year-old Japanese-born Yuji Hirayama (USA) free-climbed the Salathé in just 37 hours, with no pre-preparation and only three short falls on the Grade 5.13 pitches. Hirayama, accompanied by Hans Florine (USA) and Hidetaka Suzuki (Japan), used a 70m (230ft) rope to give longer pitches, climbing it in 23 as opposed to the usual 35-plus pitches.

In the short space of a few years, the approach to the Yosemite walls has altered radically. The challenge for the next generation has altered, but not disappeared. The 'hard men' of tomorrow can work at free-climbing all the old routes, as well as finding new lines up the valley rock.

Cerro Torre

Patagonia's Peak of Storms

Cerro Torre lies in the midst of two sets of storms – the storms which accompany its position in the windswept wildlands of Patagonia, and the storms of controversy over a number of ascents, including the reputed first ascent(s) of the peak.

Cerro Torre was labelled by climbers such as Walter Bonatti and Lionel Terray as 'impossible' and 'a scream in stone' after their 1958 attempts, largely because of the violent storms which regularly lash it. The three Torre's – Cerro, Egger and Standhardt – lie on the edge of the Southern Patagonian Ice Cap. Clear days are rare, the peak usually capped with an amazing ice mushroom. Carlo Mauri (one of Italy's leading climbers) said, after his unsuccessful attempt in 1958: 'The summit of the mountain looks like a giant cone that had been overfilled with ice cream and then pressed downwards, so that the ice cream spilled over the edges; but … had been frozen into immobility. As the west wind added more and more ice to the structure, it began to twist, and distort itself into a crazy, upside down labyrinth of ice, until gravity took over and blocks of ice the size of houses crashed down on the smooth granite walls below.' ('Cerro Torre, The West Face', *Mountain* #101, September 1970.)

THE NORTH FACE ROUTE

In January 1959, in the tenuous Patagonian summer, Toni Egger, Cesare Maestri and Cesarino Fava started up Cerro Torre, set on a fast, alpine-style ascent. After 11 days of hauling they established a

CERRO TORRE
3133m

— Northwest Ridge 1959
---- Compressor Route 1970

base on the Triangular Snowpatch. The weather changed, leading to a series of storms, and it was nearly a month before they could get back to this point. The face was now plastered with snow and ice. From the supply dump at the Snowpatch, 300m (1000ft) of fixed rope was used to reach the Col of Conquest between Cerro Torre and Torre Egger (later so named by Maestri in honour of Toni Egger), where Fava retreated of his own choice, not wishing to hold back the others. Egger and Maestri kept going, and over three days, with precarious hanging bivouacs, climbed 760m (2494ft) of steep rock and mostly ice to reach the summit. Maestri later described it: 'At each step, the whole crust made a dull noise like a low whistle, it cracked and broke and large pieces fell off. The ice pegs went in like butter, and gave us only an illusion of security. At each pitch we made a small platform, so that we could drill through into the rock, where we found not the slightest trace of a crack; so we had to drill holes for expansion bolts, and each hole needed five hundred hammer blows.' ('The Conquest of Cerro Torre, *Mountain* #81, 1968.)

As they reached the summit, a warm wind started to blow, heralding the end of the clear spell they had been lucky enough to enjoy. During the epic three-day descent in an ever-worsening storm, Egger was killed by an ice avalanche only a few pitches from safety. Fava, on the point of leaving the region, having given up hope of finding his companions, found a very weak and

Opposite The ice-plastered upper tower of the Southeast Face, controversially bolted by Maestri in 1970.
Top left Dramatic Cerro Torre, Torre Egger and Torre Standhardt stand out proudly against a rare peaceful sky.
Centre left A belay point on one of the many smaller spires to be found in the Cerro Torre Valley, Patagonia.
Bottom left Ronaldo Garibotti, a leading Italian climber, descending a couloir in a typical Patagonian storm.

confused Maestri close to the base of the route eight days after he had left the pair. Maestri, disheartened after Egger's death, had slipped on a patch of ice and tumbled the last pitch to the bottom. (In 1975 climbers found a boot, part of a leg and some clothing on the glacier – undoubtedly the remains of Toni Egger. The sole camera which would have given proof of ascending to the summit has never been found.)

Maestri's own recollection of the summit was somewhat hazy, and the climbing community was uncertain – was this a real claim, or was it made simply to honour Egger's memory, or to fuel Maestri's ego? Maestri claimed that he had placed a total of 30 bolts on the final pitches – to date, no other climbers have ever succeeded in getting anywhere near the summit on this specific route, so his claim awaits verification. Should

these bolts be found in the future, his claims would be totally vindicated, refuting his critics. The conditions on that occasion may well have been better for a rapid, ice-climbing alpine-style ascent than they have ever been since, and the pair were undoubtedly top climbers. Maestri had been known as 'the spider of the Dolomites', the name originating from his many difficult and often solo ascents there. Egger was a well-known ice

Left New Zealander Russell Braddock on the fifth pitch, Cerro Torre, on a rare fair-weather day. Laguna Torre (the usual site of base camp) lies behind him.

Above The view from the 'mushroom ridge' south of Cerro Torre, looking over the Cima Grande onto the Vledma Glacier, Southern Patagonian Ice Cap.

In the next few years many strong expeditions from a variety of countries attempted this and other routes on Cerro Torre, and they all failed, adding doubt upon doubt to Maestri's claim, and whipping up fresh storms of letters of comment among the climbing community.

The most powerful of these was the British group of Peter Crew, Martin Boysen, Mick Burke and Dougal Haston. During 1968 the team lived on the face for 30 days, and fixed hundreds of metres of rope on the first 1200m (3940ft) of the South-east Ridge, coming to within 300m (984ft) of the summit. There, they found their way blocked by blank, steep rock. Deciding that they needed more bolts, they descended, only to encounter stormy conditions for over a month. When they returned to the mountain, they found that all their ropes had been frayed by the extreme winds, and they were forced to abandon their attempt after six days.

THE COMPRESSOR ROUTE

In 1970 a still highly aggrieved Maestri returned to Cerro Torre and, in the wake of the near-success of the British team, attacked the same route, but this time brought to bear some very controversial tactics on the mountain. 'It seemed to me that the route would be impossible by normal means, so I decided that bolting would be necessary,' said Maestri. So, bolt he did. After a spell of good weather, Maestri had established himself and his team (C Claus and E Alimonta) high on the face, but storms forced them off. A month later they returned, used a helicopter to drop a wooden hut at the foot of the peak, and hauled a huge 68kg (150 lb) petrol-powered compressor to the base of, and eventually further up, the headwall – in itself a marathon feat! They then proceeded to drill and place over 300 bolts, finally reaching their high point just 18m (60ft) below the summit, at the base of the overhanging ice mushroom. For whatever reason, Maestri decided that the climb was finished, rationalizing that the mushroom 'was not rock, thus not truly part of the mountain, the true objective'. He then descended, removing many of the bolts on the top pitch.

His comments on the ascent included the following: 'If you worked in a bank, and then, just before you retired, heard a rumour that

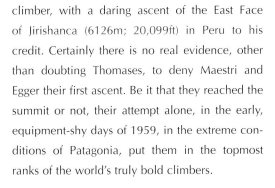

climber, with a daring ascent of the East Face of Jirishanca (6126m; 20,099ft) in Peru to his credit. Certainly there is no real evidence, other than doubting Thomases, to deny Maestri and Egger their first ascent. Be it that they reached the summit or not, their attempt alone, in the early, equipment-shy days of 1959, in the extreme conditions of Patagonia, put them in the topmost ranks of the world's truly bold climbers.

PATAGONIA

Patagonia is a most appealing destination for those climbers who love extreme conditions and stunning rock spires. Golden-brown granite, akin to the best in Chamonix or Yosemite, huge glittering fields of ice, and fairy-tale untamed rock and ice faces are offset by screaming winds, whiteouts, violent storms and months of deprivation.

Patagonia, as known and loved by climbers, runs from the lofty San Valentín (3876m; 12,520ft) – highest point on Hielo del Norte (the Northern Ice Cap) at about 45 degrees south – well into the Cordillera Darwin on Tierra del Fuego, on the other side of the Straits of Magellan.

The most famous destinations all lie along the eastern perimeter of Hielo Sur (the Southern Ice Cap), namely the Fitzroy, Cerro Torre, and Paine massifs. These mountains offer perhaps the greatest scope for alpine and super-alpine adventure in the world. In Patagonia, in addition to the prerequisite ability, experience and financial means, 'one needs a large helping of patience, an obsessive determination to succeed, a high degree of psychological resistance and a liberal helping of luck. Patagonia represents a battle against the unchained forces of nature, where diabolical winds, weather and snow conditions change with such rapidity that good sense is unable to anticipate or control the situation'. (Michel-Angel Gallego, on completion of the Spanish route, Fitzroy, 1984.)

One of the chief attractions of Patagonia is its wildness, its isolation. Climbers have to rely on their own resources – there is no convenient heli-copter rescue, à la European Alps, and civilization is a long way away. The violent, unpredictable nature of the weather adds glamour that is understandable only to the mountain extremist – a gamble with fate, of pitting oneself against odds that are heavily laden against the climber. Success becomes worthwhile by its very rareness. Many returning from a few weeks in the Pata-gonian mountains emerge in what is virtually an altered state of consciousness, and take a while to adjust to civilization. The 'wild and staring look' associated with Shakespeare's Macbeth is there, with similar memories perhaps of shrieking wind-demons, of storms and tempests, of overlong nights, and little true rest.

THE FITZROY GROUP REFLECTED IN THE LAKE AT LOS GLACIERES NATIONAL PARK, PATAGONIA.

you had walked off with US$20,000 of the bank's money … if there was some way in which you could clear your name by one theatrical gesture, would you not choose that?'

The ascent of the Compressor route brought about a fresh furore of comment; the bolt line was held as 'sacrilegious' and condemned. Expedition after expedition tried to free-climb the route, but all were compelled to use the bolt line and retreat. The line was laced with old abandoned ropes, hardware and detritus.

In 1974 a team of Italian climbers from Lecco – the 'Lecco Spiders', led by Casimiro Ferrari – climbed the West Face and Southwest Ridge. It was a difficult climb, in extreme weather conditions. Much to Maestri's ire, many claimed that this was the 'first real ascent of Cerro Torre' – discounting both of Maestri's attempts, especially the Compressor route 'because he had not climbed the ice mushroom'.

In 1979 two American climbers, Jim Bridwell and Steve Brewer, met for the first time at the base of Torre, both having been unable to find partners who were willing to risk the peak. They decided on a 'light and fast' alpine-style ascent of the Compressor route, and ended up taking two 9mm ropes, a small amount of basic climbing kit, sleeping bags, a single stove, a small bolt kit, and basic foodstuffs for three days. They climbed the first 1050m (3445ft) in an amazing single 20-hour day. The next day they headed for the summit, and Bridwell replaced the removed bolts by drilling shallow holes for aluminium rivets, and placing marginal pitons and copperheads in the cracks. He and Brewer eventually reached and surmounted the ice mushroom, summitting in 90kph (56mph) winds. They reached the base the same day, after a series of hair-raising abseils, including one where Bridwell fell 40m (130ft) after a sling broke. The Compressor route had been climbed, largely free, and 'properly summitted'.

A number of hard routes have been established on Cerro Torre, Torre Egger, and Torre Standhardt (which was the last to succumb, in 1988, to a USA team of Jim Bridwell, and J and G Smith). Virtually all Torre routes (as do most in Patagonia) require great skill in free rock climbing, aid climbing, and water ice (ice climbing).

Cerro Torre still lures top climbers from around the world – it offers extreme challenges, including the tantalizing lure of Maestri's original North Face route, as well as a number of incomplete routes on the remote, weatherbeaten West Face.

Maestri's compressor still hangs on its chains, an idiosyncratic monument to the epic history of this peak, marking the bolted line of the Compressor route. This route, despite its critics, has seen its top bolt ladder used as a finishing line to a number of other fine routes, and has saved countless lives by offering a relatively safe and easy descent in poor conditions.

The climbing community eagerly awaits a second ascent of the disputed first ascent line, with some record of Maestri and Egger's bolts still in place, which would vindicate a man who for many is still a hero.

Below left Climbing the Towers of Paine – loose flakes of granite, icy handholds and perpetual steepness are an accepted part of the game in Patagonia.

Below The imposing Towers of Paine – North, Central and South (left to right) – are yet another prime mountaineering target.

Polar Sun Spire

The Great and Secret Show

The Great and Secret Show was 'secret' – almost. In June 1995, Warren Hollinger (USA), Mark Synott (USA) and Jerry Gore (UK) explored a small area on Baffin Island, just south of the Arctic Circle, and discovered countless superb walls tucked away in hidden fjords, some previously only seen by Inuit hunters (*see* page 123). In the three 'terra incognita' fjords the climbing trio briefly explored, 300m (1000ft) walls were numerous, 600m (2000ft) giants commonplace, 900m (3000ft) monsters numbered at least 10, and the adjacent Clark Fjord had a 1220m (4000ft) free-standing pillar. The virgin rock of Polar Sun Spire stood out above the rest, with the 1340m (4400ft) North Face rising from the sea in a great sweep of rock, possibly the greatest vertical cliff in the world. The excited trio attempted this, but poor rock on their chosen route scared them off after 200m (700ft). They returned in 1996, Gore having been replaced by Jeff Chapman. Unfortunately their 'secret' had leaked out, and a Japanese team arrived at the same time. In the words of Hollinger, 'They [the Japanese] were so dead set on Polar Sun Spire that they fixed the first 300m (1000ft) of a route to the left of ours, in anticipation of returning next year. We were a little bummed to be sharing the wall when there was so much virgin rock in the area, but the Japanese left the fjord after only two weeks.' After that, the US team had it all to themselves.

'Great' the route certainly was – it turned out to be the biggest Arctic wall ever tackled, and led to climbing of a sustained and serious nature. The

— *Polar Sun Spire, North Face, 1996*

weather was bleak, with a surface temperature of 0°C (32°F) excluding the wind-chill factor brought about by the constant high winds. The group was worried about the portaledge surviving. Should this (their sole shelter on the rock face) rip, or should they drop vital equipment, they '… could end up as a belay Popsicle', to quote Synott. As Hollinger put it, 'The nearest rescue is in New York City.' The portaledge, with its one-person attachment (Little Rico) dangling below it, was the sole 'comfort' they would have for 39 days on the wall. The weather was often so bad that the group could not even stir from the portaledges, which did not allow sitting up, or even turning on one's side. Some 20 of the 29 days were storm filled, temperatures averaging well below freezing. The portaledge even required 'taking a leak' lying down – a messy situation as can be imagined! Cooking was a trial, and fraught with the danger of setting the whole show alight in the climbers' buffeting little nylon cocoons.

The route began as a near-vertical 300m (1000ft) buttress on the right of the amphitheatre, leading to a huge snow ledge below the main wall. Five days later, with a few hundred kilograms of gear hauled up, the team were ready for the next section, dubbed The Arch Enemy – a series of curving corner cracks that angled up leftwards through the granite for 150m (500ft). The belayer often had to endure 10–15 hours of deep-frozen belaying, unable to relax his vigilance, or even move. The pattern was: climb for as long as

Opposite A daunting view of the vast vertical sea of frozen granite which houses The Great and Secret Show.
Top right Jumaring up the bottom third of the route, just before the section called The Arch Enemy.
Centre right A rock climber contending with a tangle of gear – big wall climbing requires a cool head.
Bottom right The 'bat tent' dangles precariously over the huge and steep expanse of the Polar Sun Spire.

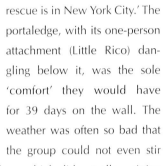

Left A view down to the fjord – the climbers keep a nervous eye on the still-frozen ice.

Below The Polar Sun Spire rises like a giant ship from the icy waters of Baffin Island.

picked up food, fuel and water, and headed up the jumar again. It took two days to get the 275kg (600 lb) load up the 500m (1700ft) of fixed ropes.

For two weeks they climbed up vertical or overhanging rock, with no snow to melt for water. At last, with only a few litres left, they found a snow-filled ledge. They experienced the problems of living shoulder-to-shoulder in tough conditions – verbal scraps, moroseness, and 'lows' of emotion.

'Perched on a sea cliff without a single other person within 130km (80 miles), the feeling of self-reliance was intense, and empowering. The sense of commitment, which could sometimes bring me so low, now gave me resolve to deal with the strains of wall life.' (Synott: 'The Great and Secret Show', *American Alpine Club Journal*, 1997.)

At last they summitted the final Yosemite-crack-style headwall, with its immaculate hand and chimney cracks. 'We had been attached to each other like Siamese triplets for more than a month of sickness. At times I had asked myself: "Which partner do I want to kill first?" We had driven each other into foaming-at-the-mouth fits, but these epics seem like nothing now. We danced a jig, arm in arm, on the summit block.' (Ibid.)

The group made their exit before the ice break-up and left behind a significant new route. Baffin Island will doubtless increase in popularity among climbers, its walls challenging those hardy enough to risk them. But the Great and Secret Show will remain one of the test pieces for years to come.

possible, then fix the rope to a solid anchor on the high point, abseil to the portaledges, 'jug' (jumar) up the rope to the high point (belayer and leader), then repeat until the high point is 200m (700ft) above the portaledges. Haul the portaledges to the high point. Repeat. (This is 'capsule-style' climbing – everything accompanies the group all the way up.) The technique works – until something runs out. In this case, it was water. Eleven days

and 520m (1700ft) up the wall the group realized their fuel was running out – water was freezing almost as soon as they melted it, and melting ice is fuel-hungry. They were running late – it was 6 June, and the pick-up by the Inuit was scheduled for 16 June. Soon the ice might begin to break up, and the fjord would become difficult to access. The team had no choice – they abseiled to base camp, radioed in that they needed a bit more time,

BAFFIN ISLAND ~ *OIKIJKTALUK*

Tucked between Greenland and Hudson Bay to the northeast of Canada is the large, irregular landmass of Baffin Island, with the Cumberland Sound taking a huge bite out of the south coast, and the northern tip nudging the Arctic Circle. Baffin Island has a rare, wild and unspoiled beauty, forgotten by time and neglected by modern man. It has large glaciers in its centre, tumbling to the sea through narrow fjords hedged with granite spires that dwarf even Yosemite's immense walls.

Most of the approaches to the mountains are done using skidoos (powered sledges) and boats, the peaks often being ascended directly from sea level (or rather, ice level). It is still sparsely populated by the Inuit (Eskimo) tribe, who, like the Sherpas of the Himalayas, are struggling to come to grips with the 'civilization' being thrust upon them. The Inuits are starting to do business guiding and resupplying climbers and explorers — the trade-off is the hugely increased incidence of venereal diseases, tuberculosis, alcoholism and other 'Western ills'.

This is typical Arctic land — high winds, freezing weather, long summer days, longer winter nights. Baffin Island was first described in the late 1500s, with coastal exploration in the early 1600s credited to William Baffin (UK), after whom the island was named. Only in the 20th century has the rugged interior been explored; the peaks saw little exploration in this harsh and unforgiving land until the highest peak, Tête Blanche (2156m; 7073ft), was climbed by a Swiss expedition in 1953.

Not the highest, but certainly the most spectacular peak is Mount Asgard (2011m; 6598ft), the South Peak of which was climbed by Guy Lee (UK), Phil Kock and Rob Wood (Canada) via the South Buttress in 1971. The Anglo-American team consisting of Doug Scott, Dennis Hennek, Paul Braithwaite and Paul Nunn climbed the more difficult North Peak at Grade 5.8 via the East Face in a 35-hour nonstop climb in 1972. The climb was on immaculate granite, and finished up a stunning tower, riven by a perfect chimney crack.

In 1975 Charlie Porter (USA) did an amazing 40-pitch solo ascent of a new Grade VI route on Mount Asgard's North Tower. It took him a month to ferry equipment in to the base, and after his successful but storm-filled climb, he hiked out over 10 days, without food or fuel. Glowing reports of the scores of 1000m-high (3300ft) pristine granite walls on this and other peaks that were just waiting for first ascents started a series of pilgrimages to this area. These included a full film crew, to film Rick Sylvester's ski-parachute jump off Asgard's summit (best known as the escape scene of the James Bond movie On Her Majesty's Secret Service*). A number of excellent climbs have since been opened.*

BAFFIN ISLAND PEAKS, VIEW NEAR TASUIT SPIRE. THE IMPOSING NATURE OF THE WALLS TUG AT THE HEART OF ANY CLIMBER WHO IS WILLING TO CLIMB IN THESE FREEZING CONDITIONS.

THE PROVING GROUND

THE PROVING GROUND

ICE CLIMBING • ROCK CLIMBING • SPORT CLIMBING

A great number of the climbs previously discussed have been done with the object (at least on the first ascent) of providing a route to the top of a peak or summit which could not have been reached by other means (short of the ultimate cheat – a helicopter).

Not all climbing is about multi-day struggles with uncomfortable bivouacs and the threat of death or danger in order to reach the top of an unknown peak – a good deal is done purely for fun. Early Scottish climbers pioneered the ice climbs on Ben Nevis for the sake of excitement. Rock climbers climb for the pure joy of movement, or to 'be with nature' or just 'for the heck of it'. In sport climbing the goal is even more obscure: why spend 17 months to complete a route up only 10m (30ft) of overhanging rock next to a smelly canal?

No climbing is without danger, and climbers have died in pursuit of their passion at all levels of the sport, though fewer in sport climbing than any other branch – a logical 'new age' development?

This is not to say that the activities described are risk free. In particular, modern mixed ice climbing, as practised by exponents such as Canadian Alex Lowe, on routes such as his aptly named Troubled Dreams, M7+, is hard and dangerous. 'A fall might kind of end it', says Joe Josephson, author of *Sea of Vapours*. Long lead-outs on thin, fragile ice columns or sheets, balanced delicately on the tips of crampons, dependant on the minutest points of two ice axes, or scrabbling frantically with sparking crampon points on rock, with marginal protection far below – this is serious climbing indeed.

Similarly, attempts on pure rock routes such as those put up by Johnny Dawes in Wales – Indian Face (E9 6c) or 'deathwish territory' – and Master's Wall, E7 6b, by Leo Houlding (*see* page 137), epitomize climbers willing to take risks for their sport.

Areas offering exciting climbing are scattered all over, including the Bugaboos (British Columbia, USA) with their numerous granite spires (although these might well be classed as Alpine routes, many are one-day climbs which can be approached without ice gear). Some that catch the fancy are the 1981 All along the Watchtower (VI, 5.10, A2) on North Howser Spire, and the 1994 Young Men on Fire (VI, 5.11, A4, with free lightning bolts thrown in) of Warren Hollinger (USA) and Jerry Gore (UK).

One cannot forget the efforts of climbers such as Catherine Destivelle, regularly climbing hard grades, or Lynn Hill with routes such as Running Man (5.13d) in the Shawangunks; nor Tony Yaniro with his Grand Illusion (5.13b) in 1979 and Closing Down (5.14a) at Mount Charleston in 1994.

Many areas deserve a mention – for instance the Italian–Austrian Dolomites, with stunning spires and walls, such as the Tre Cima de Laveredo, or the Marmalado North Faces, the Sella Towers, the Brenta – all wonderful 'playgrounds' for climbers. Many older aid routes still await free ascents, and challenges exist for generations to come.

The 'New Worlds' – Australia, Namibia, South Africa, Zimbabwe, South America (particularly the east coast) – offer rock climbs in exotic settings (after all, it is special to lie in your tent while a lion roars nearby, or a kangaroo munches your rope…).

Previous pages Huw Widdowson on Scourge, Mount Arapiles, a forging ground of Australian climbing.
Opposite El Matador, Devil's Tower, Wyoming, became the first national monument in the USA in 1906.
Top right Ice climbing is becoming an increasingly popular activity among climbers who enjoy a challenge.

BEN NEVIS
Location: Scotland
Summit height: 1344m (4406ft)

DINAS CROMLECH
Location: Llanberis Pass, Wales
Length: 40m (130ft)

CLOGWYN DU'R ARDDU
Location: Snowdon, Wales
Length: 70m (230ft)

SUPER CRACK
Location: Utah, USA
Length: 100m (300ft)

THE NAKED EDGE
Location: Redgarden Wall, Colorado, USA
Length: 200m (660ft)

THE DIAMOND
Location: Long's Peak, Colorado, USA
Length: 600m (2000ft)

OZYMANDIAS
Location: Mount Buffalo, Australia
Length: 270m (880ft)

THE BARD
Location: Mount Arapiles, Australia
Length: 120m (390ft)

ACTION DIRECTE
Location: Frankenjura, Germany
Length: 10m (30ft)

OPEN AIR
Location: Schleier Wasserfallen, Austria
Length: 50m (150ft)

Ice Climbing

The Glass Wall Game

It is probably safe to say that the roots of modern ice climbing go back to Scotland in the late 1800s. This is not to say that ice was not climbed before then – it was, particularly in the European Alps, where major (and minor) ascents could not have taken place without a good deal of skill being exercised on ice. The European guides in particular became skilful snow and ice climbers.

But ice climbing in its own right, where the object of the exercise was to ascend a short, hard icefall or gully for no other reason than to complete it, found its origins in the cold, harsh Scottish Highlands. The usual highlight of such a climb was the entertainment provided by the climber's penetration of the top cornice.

In 1870 Bill Haskett-Smith and his companions boldly forged their way up Number 3 Gully on Ben Nevis, the crucible of ice climbing in the British Isles. Today regarded as a 'stroll', it is rated as a Grade I in ice climbs. In 1870, however, there were no crampons, no ice screws, and no protection from the rope. Climbing was done by the laborious and precarious process of cutting steps, and in the early days the routes inevitably followed the gullies. The specially placed 'nails' in the boots gave a touch of grip on hard ice. Slowly the activity gained a following, and in 1893 W Naismith published *Snowcraft in Scotland*, for many years the handbook for ice climbers.

BEN NEVIS 1344m

—— Zero Gully 1957
----- Point 5 Gully 1959
– – – Orion Face Direct 1960

In 1894 a team led by Professor Collie ascended Ben Nevis' 600m (2000ft) Tower Ridge – a formidable Grade III climb, which pointed the future way to escaping from the gullies and tackling the faces.

The next major innovation came when crampons, used in various rather inefficient forms by European shepherds but regarded with suspicion by the 'real climbers', were redesigned by the innovative Oscar Eckenstein to fasten effectively under the whole sole of the boot. This led to a spate of climbs that took place just before, and again after, World War I. Shorter axes were gradually coming into play, and then the real revolution came with the adoption of 'front points' on the crampons and rigid-soled boots which allowed climbers literally to 'walk up' vertical ice.

Advances in ropes as well as in ice and rock protection gave rise to several attempts on harder and more ambitious routes, and as a result the winter mountains became the favoured playground of a new breed of 'hard men' – the ice climbers. The American, Yvon Chouinard, and Scotland's 'climbing engineer', Hamish MacInnes, independently of each other forged short, all-metal ice axes with the aggressively down-curved picks that still hold sway today, leading to the 'dagger' and 'front-point' techniques in common use nowadays. MacInnes' 'Terrodactyls' pointed the way for future technical ice axes.

Opposite Todd Cozzens climbing the vertical frozen waterfall Dressed to Kill in Cody, Wyoming, USA.
Top left This climber is pictured ascending Point 5 Gully, Ben Nevis – the epitome of Scottish ice climbing.
Centre left Hamish MacInnes, renowned Scottish mountaineer, uses Terrodactyl ice tools, his own invention.
Bottom left Crampon points and axe tips keep this climber on the South Face of Mount Hicks, New Zealand.

BEN NEVIS

The Scottish Highlands – one of the greatest wilderness areas in Western Europe – cover one-fifth of the land area of the United Kingdom. They lie on the same cold northern latitude as Labrador. There are many spectacular and difficult climbs on the 543 summits of over 900m (3000ft), but the gem in the crown is Ben Nevis ('Nevis' meaning 'hellish' in Gaelic). At 1342m (4406ft) it is the highest peak in the British Isles, and boasts Tower Ridge, a magnificent north-facing amphi-theatre with miles of cliffs and gullies that reach as high as 600m (2000ft). It is a meeting ground for scores of climbers, with ample good rock in the summer months, and countless gullies and ice waterfalls during the winter. Although Scotland has a great number of fine crags, such as Buachaille Etive Mor in Glen Coe, 'The Ben' is where it all began.

Two of the great lines on Ben Nevis were the coveted Point 5 and Zero gullies, lying on either side of Observatory Ridge, a rock buttress that was climbed in 1901 by the 'father' of Scottish climbing, Harold Raeburn, as a solo rock climb, and again in 1920 as the first winter ice ascent. Climbers eyed the two fine gully lines, but

Above Zero Gully, Ben Nevis – the goal of many an ice climber in Scotland.

Below The Lochaber Mountain Rescue team evacuates a casualty in Number 3 Gully on Ben Nevis.

common sense usually prevailed, and attempts were staved off until the mid-1950s. Zero Gully was the first to have a full ascent, in 1958.

Zero Gully

'Whoever christened it a gully was an optimist. For 120 metres it is no more than a vertical corner bulging with overhangs.' (Tom Patey, on the first ascent, in the *Scottish Mountaineering Club Journal*, May 1958).

The climb starts with 35m (120ft) of 85-degree ice in a narrow trough, leading to an 'ominous' overhang. 'The technique is to take tension through an ice piton placed as high as possible above the climber until the next few handholds have been cut. Then, hanging on with one hand, a higher piton is inserted and the lower one taken out for re-use. This is all very delicate work, as any out-ward pull on the piton will have the maximum result'. (Ibid) The precarious ice screw placements are a notorious feature of Zero Gully. ('Zero stands for Zero protection', is the common complaint, though the name is credited as having arisen from MacInnes' habit of saying: 'Zero Hour – let's go!')

MacInnes and Robert Hope had retreated on a previous occasion, following 'a wee avalanche' which hit them after they had completed the first 130m (400ft) of the route. MacInnes, Patey and A Nicol, the trio who completed the first ascent of Zero Gully in 1957, followed the same thin strand of ice upwards over bulge after bulge, sometimes progressing in a frenzy of free climbing, some-times relying on virtual aid techniques to get over the smooth, hard, steep ice. Eventually, after five cold hours, they had climbed the four or five pitches that constitute the forest of overhangs, then they completed the last five pitches to the summit cornice, and through this onto the summit in less than an hour.

Point 5 Gully

'A hard Grade V indeed!' was MacInnes' descrip-tion of Point 5 Gully. Officially graded the same as Zero Gully, few would argue with the truth of that statement. What makes Point 5 'more significant' than many other climbs of similar grade is the huge cornice which usually hangs over it in the winter months and is intermittently prone to avalanching pieces of itself down the route.

Above Traversing on Orion Face Direct – even direct routes on the Ben often require some back-and-forth searching.

Right Climbing on thin water ice requires the deft and precise use of axe and crampons, as pictured here on Hadrian's Wall, Ben Nevis.

First summitted in 1959 by I Clough, J Alexander, D Pipes and R Shaw, Point 5 Gully's final ascent required 29 solid hours of siege-type climbing, spread out over a five-day period. Each pitch was hard and sustained, either just off vertical or over-hanging; each move required care and thought. Clough described it as a 'wicked jigsaw', and others have described the route as 'vertical chess' – each move has to be planned well in advance.

Near the top the gully narrows to a tiny icicle crammed between blocks of rock which, although forcing the climber to do mixed climbing, at least allows for some solid protection in the adjacent rock. 'Mixed' climbing is when the ice thinly overlays or lies adjacent to rock, forcing the climber to climb rock and ice with crampons on. Much of the winter climbing done in Scotland (and elsewhere) is 'mixed' in that conditions vary from year to year, and highly iced routes one year may have merely a thin coating the next. It all adds to the excitement, as the locals say.

After this hard narrow gully, the route leads right into the fearsome cornice, which is either 'burrowed' or 'scuttled' – that is, the bold plough straight through it, while the more prudent move towards Observatory Ridge and turn the cornice where it is less threatening. Needless to say, the first ascensionists did not scuttle!

Rock Climbing

The Technicians of the Sacred

In most aspects of climbing, right up to the huge Himalayan peaks, there is some actual climbing on rock involved. This may be as small as the short rock band on the North Ridge of Everest, or extended, as in the Kangshung Face. In these cases, the rock is merely another in a series of obstacles to be overcome – snow, ice, altitude, winds, cold – and the rock climbing is not an end in itself.

However, there are countless areas of the world where rock climbing is practised as the sole obstacle, and the object of the climbing is seldom to reach the top of a 'peak', only the top of a particular band of rock. Perhaps this might be thought to lack the grandeur of alpine, big wall or high mountain ascents, but it is a popular and widely practised sport, and not without its dangers. Many rock climbers have died in the pursuit of their goal – some by unavoidable accidents, some by carelessness, and many in climbing 'free' (unroped) solo routes. One can no more criticize those who take these risks than one can a sky-diver, a formula-one driver or a top cyclist. The nature of any high-level game at the 'cutting edge' involves a measure of risk.

It is truly impossible to choose one rock climb as the 'top climb'; it is not even possible to choose one country or area as the birthplace of modern rock climbing. Rather, a sampling of magnificent climbs from a variety of countries are included to give a taste of what pure rock climbing involves.

– – Cemetery Gates 1951
- - - Cenotaph Corner 1952
——— Left Wall 1970
····· Lord of the Flies 1979

DINAS CROMLECH

If any place deserves the accolade of being the birthplace of the sport of climbing short rock routes, it is probably Britain, with the Welsh hills of the Llanberis Pass as its cradle.

High above the narrow, steep road that winds among green, sheep-filled pastures interspersed with crags and mountain streams, lies a rock feature that immediately catches the eye of the climber: a huge, open-book wall, two blank faces joining at right angles with a vivid crack-line. This is Dinas Cromlech, and in its span of 50x50m (150x150ft) lie some of the world's best climbs, bearing evocative names like Cenotaph Corner, Cemetery Gates, and Lord of the Flies.

In Britain, climbing started off largely as a 'gentleman's sport'. After World War II, a new force entered the arena – the working class, who had time and energy to spare. The most famous of these was Joe Brown, a Manchester-born plumber (called the 'human spider') and a living legend who still climbs hard routes in his late sixties! In 1948 he was 18, impetuous and daring. Cenotaph Corner had repulsed dozens of parties – it was considered 'beyond sane limits' for the equipment and techniques of the time. Joe Brown started up it with a heavy Manila rope tied loosely around his waist, a stonemason's hammer, five chunky metal home-forged pegs, a few tied-off slings, and a number of heavy steel carabiners. He hoped to be

Opposite The limestone cliffs of the Verdon Gorge in southern France are a playground for the rock climber.

Top right A climber approaching the crux moves on Cenotaph Corner, a rock climb at Dinas Cromlech.

Centre right Classic bridging moves at the start of the elegant Cenotaph Corner in Llanberis Pass, Wales.

Bottom right The Left Wall at Dinas Cromlech, a test-piece route requiring a delicate technique.

Opposite The evocative 'open book' corner and steep flanking walls of Dinas Cromlech.

Top Denise belays her mother, guide Brede Arkless, on the airy second pitch of Cemetery Gates.

Above A young Joe Brown on the cliffs of Craig Gogarth, near North Stack lighthouse.

Right A female climber leading the sustained crux section of Left Wall, Dinas Cromlech.

able to stick a peg in every 8m (20ft) or so, and loop a sling around the odd rock spike. The rest is legend – at 27m (90ft) Joe hammered in one peg, put the hammer in his mouth to free his hands for clipping the rope, then yelled to his belayer, Wilf White, for slack. He forgot just one little thing ... The hammer hit Wilf on the head, and knocked him out cold. Joe Brown, appalled, untied himself from the rope and descended hand over hand. When the bleeding Wilf came around, all he growled at Brown was: 'Get back there and do the bloody thing!' So that is what he did – almost.

Near the top he ran out of pegs and decided to retreat. Sadly he had to wait two and a half years for a rematch with the climb.

When Brown came back, he 'zipped up the climb in a flash', astounding all the local climbers. The crux move comes two-thirds of the way up, where the crack widens and goes through a tiny overhang. The tough and determined Brown flung himself at this move so fast that he was nearly pulled right off, his belayer not being quick enough to feed out rope. It is claimed, probably accurately, that Joe Brown and his band of fellow climbers,

which included Don Whillans, spurred rock climbing to new levels of difficulty worldwide.

Climbing history was once again made on Dinas Cromlech in 1979, when Ron Fawcett, one of the world's top climbers, did a first ascent of the steep line up the wall to the right of Cenotaph – Lord of the Flies, graded E6 6a (5.12c). What made this ascent different was that it was being filmed by BBC TV. 'I couldn't even fookin' swear!' said Fawcett later. The tension of a first-time climb is admirably caught in the film, where a single mistake could have plunged Fawcett to the ground.

CLOGWYN DU'R ARDDU

Set back on the opposite side of Llanberis Pass from Dinas Cromlech is a far larger and more brooding crag, Clogwyn du'r Arddu, or 'Cloggy', as it is commonly called. This huge, curved amphitheatre lies high on the North Face of a summit ridge leading out from Snowdon, the highest point in Wales. It was the scene of the first publicly recorded rock climb in Britain, when two ministers, the reverends Bingley and Williams, got lost in their ardent search for botanical specimens in 1798 and ended up climbing the East Terrace (with a good deal of trepidation, one might read in their account). Cloggy was fairly quiet for a while after that, until over 100 years later a series of almost insanely bold young climbers – such as Colin Kirkus, the climbing poet Geoffrey Winthrop-Young, the young George Mallory and the melancholy and manic-depressive John Menlove Edwards –

‐ ‐ ‐ *Vember 1951* ····· *Masters Wall 1986*
—— *Great Wall 1975*

pioneered all the most obvious crack and arête routes (*see* page 159) on the magnificent crag.

This left the faces – long, blank, mildly overhanging and very, very sparse on protection. The Great Wall, 70m (230ft) of serious climbing, was opened at E4 6a (5.11) – an amazing grade for

Above Clogwyn du'r Arddu on the northwest flank of Mount Snowdon. The Great Wall is half in shadow, but even in full light this imposing crag has a sombre, sobering effect on climbers.

1962 – by Peter Crew, using 'just a tiny bit of aid'. Youth had its say about this state of affairs when the 16-year-old John Allen finally climbed it free in 1975. In 1986 another 'young pretender' came to Cloggy – the dynamic young Johnny Dawes, in his early 20s. He climbed directly up the fingernail cracks and matchbox-sized ledges on the unprotected East Face of Cloggy, to open the famed Indian Face, a direct and uncompromising route of unheard-of difficulty and danger. A fall onto the purely psychological protection of the tiny number one RP (a minute metal wedge) high up on the climb would have brought certain death, and the route was graded E9 6c (5.14) –

Right Often dubbed the most influential climber of the decade, the legendary Jerry Moffat is pictured here on Master's Edge, Sheffield, England (not to be confused with Master's Wall in Wales).

the first E9 in Britain. The route understandably remained unrepeated for many years, and in fact still awaits an on-sight (*see* page 159) ascent.

In the 1980s a controversial figure emerged on the world climbing scene – Jerry Moffat, who was challenging the great Ron Fawcett. Moffat was classed as a 'superbrat' – supremely self-confident, brash and, to top it all, damnably successful! In 1983 Fawcett had put up a superbly difficult, pro-tectionless climb up a steep, off-balance arête at the gritstone quarry of Millstone, called Master's Edge, graded E7 6a. Moffat retaliated with his own E7 6b – he completed the tough line of tiny sloping edges and minute finger cracks that make up the 45m (150ft) of Cloggy's Master's Wall, thereby thumbing his nose at the older establishment.

The route saw only three repeat ascents in 14 years, all extensively practised on top rope, before the young Leo Houlding stood before it in 1997. Truly lionesque in his boldness, he had never set foot or hand on the climb. He decided to take on Cloggy, and stunned the climbing world with a bold, scary on-sight lead – that of Master's Wall, graded at E7 6b (5.12d). He was just 16, and the route terrified most adult climbers – his suc-cessful lead certainly put the wind up the older climbers in the world – par for the course for Master's Wall which itself arose out of a quiet feud for supremacy. Realizing that his shoes had worn through, Houlding borrowed a pair from his belayer, whose feet were sadly 'a bit large'. The role of pre-cise footwork on a climb such as Master's Wall is vital, and he started at a disadvantage that would have caused most climbers to call it off. Time was short, so the impetuous youngster just went for it.

The route is by no means simple – it has an abundance of twists and turns, with numerous subtle, invisible side-pulls, misleading flakes that dead-end, and protection that is all but entirely impossible to find. After approximately 20m (70ft) Houlding came to a complete stop, and stood where he was for about 20 minutes – precariously perched on the minutest of hand-

and footholds, quite a long way above his last none too solid protection – contemplating the crux series of moves. By this stage of the climb the small group of onlookers in attendance had 'all ceased to even breathe'. No one dared to say a word and thereby disturb his concentration.

He finally started off, then his feet slipped and, by 'fate or good fortune' (according to Houlding himself), he lunged for and managed to find the tiny key hold. After that, it was plain sailing, to give what ranks as one of the boldest on-sight natural-gear leads to date.

SUPER CRACK

The desert areas of America bring to mind the cowboy films with which many of us grew up – endless pastel-coloured landscapes, miles of barren sand broken by the occasional bush, ringed by towering rock spires and long, threatening canyons. Utah has thousands of square kilometres of this kind of terrain. Tucked away in Indian Creek Canyon is one of America's most famous crack lines – Super Crack (5.10). The USA's Ed Webster, who was on the opening ascent, described Super Crack as follows: 'Even in my wildest dreams, I'd never imagined such a crack, a fissure so parallel-walled, so eye-catchingly

Left Earl Wiggins belays Ed Webster on the first ascent of Super Crack, Indian Creek Canyon, Utah.

straight, so perfect! Here was a crack so flawless God must have sliced it on a lucky day in Heaven.' (Chris Jones, *Climbing in North America*, American Alpine Club, 1976.)

In 1976, when Webster, Jim Dunn, Earl Wiggins and Bryan Becker (all USA) tackled the 100m (300ft) clean-cut sandstone crack, protection was limited to huge 'bongs' (hollow metal tubes and wedges), pitons or even wooden wedges – none of today's expanding camming devices that help to protect parallel-sided cracks. 'The sandstone was soft enough that, if the leader fell, there was the probability that a lot of the nuts would shear out of the crack, and the leader hit the ground.' (Ibid.)

Super Crack has the most magnificent 'jams' imaginable – every kind of jam, from finger to fist to arm to off-width (a crack that is too wide to lock an arm or leg in, but too narrow to insert the whole body into it; climbed by a technique amusingly known as 'struggle and pray', one wriggles up such a crack as best one can). The group boldly worked its way up the intricate sequence of jams, using the immaculate crack to its fullest extent. They managed to avoid any falls and thereby succeeded in establishing one of the top routes in the area – still regarded as one of the best of the many outstanding crack lines for which the region is renowned.

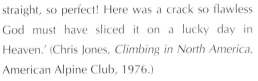

Above Earl Wiggins getting to grips with the overlap on the first ascent of Super Crack.

Right top and bottom Note the 'torqueing' of feet in the cracks – a painful but essential technique.

THE NAKED EDGE

The area around the aptly named Boulder, Colorado, has a multitude of cliffs, large and small. The Rocky Mountain National Park lies 48km (30 miles) away, with the impressive Long's Peak (4344m; 14,255ft) dominating. The East Face offers 600m (2000ft) of vertical and overhanging rock, including the famous Diamond. The whole area is riddled with canyons, some with walls over 600m (2000ft) high. Just 12km (8 miles) south of Boulder lies the Eldorado Springs Canyon, pre-eminent in the development of American rock climbing. Redgarden Wall has been likened to Cloggy, and has played a similar role in raising free climbing standards.

The 200m (600ft) of Redgarden Wall leans skyward in a formidable array of stepped overhangs, intricate cracks and vertical walls. It has layers of red, orange and white rock interspersed with brown slabs overlaid with the bright yellow of lichens. Up until 1956 no one gave serious consideration to climbing it, until four Colorado climbers – Chuck Murley, Cary Huston, Dick Bird and Dallas Jackson – gave it a go. On their third attempt they opened a line up a series of off-balance slabs and ramps, giving 'Redguard' a 5.7 – a 'jolly good grade' for those days. The first pitch, named The Birdcage, still catches climbers by surprise by its off-balance nature which tends to 'barndoor' them off – that is, force them away from the cliff.

During the early 1960s, the overhanging prow on the right-hand side of Redgarden caught the eye of many of the top climbers, all of whom attempted it, all of whom were repulsed. One of these was the incredibly talented Layton Kor (USA) who had started off a shy, tall individual, bouldering solo on some extremely hard routes. The locals had even placed bets on how long he was going to live (three months was the longest estimate). The gangly Kor was to become the Joe Brown of Colorado, influencing climbing for decades to come. He persuaded Steve Komito, a local cobbler, to accompany him on his first

-- *The Naked Edge* —— *Redguard Route* ···· *T2*

attempt. They 'nailed' (aided) up the first crack, then headed on to a slab that had turned back a number of other parties. Kor got into trouble halfway across, and petrified the inexperienced Komito by screaming that he was going to come off and take them both down! Somehow Kor lowered himself off, and the pair beat a dishevelled retreat.

Kor was back, in 1962, with Chouinard's new pitons, developed in Yosemite. The first pitch went as planned, the second at A4 (a very serious aid grade in the 1960s, as it is now) was forced between the troublesome slab and the huge overhangs, and then they were forced off to a dihedral (*see* page 159) on the left of the final arête. The Naked Edge had been completed, but was not yet finished.

In the 1970s the emphasis changed from aiding to freeing. The advent of lighter, stronger ropes, harnesses sturdy enough to take falls, and more sophisticated protection opened the way for more

Far left Ian Spencer-Green on Cassandra (5.12d), Penitente Canyon, Colorado.

Left Ian Spencer-Green on A Virgin No More (5.12c/d), Penitente Canyon, Colorado.

Below Fred Knapp on Dawn of an Age (5.10b), Blue Grama Cliff, Indian Creek, Utah.

Right The upper reaches of the Naked Edge, showing the key traversing ledge sloping off leftwards.

elegant approaches to the rock. The scarring of rock by hard pitons was considered environmentally unsound; chalk and sticky rubber rock boots arrived instead, leaving less serious markings.

There were 'big names' in Colorado at that time – Jim Erickson was a determined climber, as was Steve Wunsch. Both were incredibly fit and bold – characteristics essential for their target, a free climb of the Naked Edge. Erickson made many attempts with various partners, including his brother Dave, but always fell off. In 1971, he and Steve Wunsch got together. In Erickson's laconic words: 'Steve and I sit in Boulder trying to consume enough pancakes and coffee to achieve consciousness. Yesterday we completed the third free ascent of Country Club Crack. Today we are poised for a presumptuous attempt on the Naked Edge, a spectacular classic regardless of how it is climbed. Five times failure so far, no reason today will be different. Steve is excited to try, and needs someone to humour him, and belay.'

They managed the lower sections, even though one short 5.10 section took an hour. Then, disappointment. It was getting dark, and neither had the energy to tackle the final outward-leaning edge. Retreat was inevitable. Wunsch left for Yosemite.

But Erickson was back the next weekend, with Duncan Ferguson. They could race up the first pitches now, as the sequence was clear in Erickson's memory. They rested for an hour on a tiny belay platform, then Erickson headed out onto the battleship bow. 'Strenuous, overhanging finger-laybacking leads around a corner. A severely overhanging hand-crack pierces the prow, leading thirty feet upward and out of sight. My forearms feel like melted silly-putty, light years of emptiness beneath. I have but strength for one attempt.'

Three metres of outward hand-jamming climbing led him to a fixed peg, then another three to near the edge of the overhang, and another peg.

'Both hands slip from the crack, the next heartbeat extends for eternity. I instinctively grab the edge of the crack with both hands for a quasi-layback; pull with everything there is left, and lunge forever into a perfect hand-slot with my left hand. It crunches into the crack and grinds to a stop, ripping skin as my weight puts its strength to trial, preventing a breathtakingly long fall.'

Erickson reached the top. The climb was given 'solid 5.10' in the days when 5.10 was the highest grade thought possible – today it is regarded as a solid 5.11. In 1978, Jim Collins (USA) decided to try it as a free solo. He had climbed it five times, and said, 'I had only done the fifth, overhanging hand-jam pitch once without falling off. There were three thoughts in my mind as I started the pitch – one, I didn't want to do it. Another was that I did want to do it. Another thought was that I just didn't care. It wasn't a suicidal thing. I started up the hand-crack thinking that I would just go for a really solid-looking fixed pin, and then clip into it and wait for a rescue. But every time I got to a pin I trusted my climbing ability more than just one pin, and so I would keep going.' He finished the route.

Whatever the grade and style, the Naked Edge is a true classic, a superb climb in a superb setting.

THE DIAMOND

If any piece of rock can be said to 'cry out for an ascent', it is the Diamond on the East Face of Long's Peak in Colorado's Rocky Mountain National Park. By 1938 numerous routes had been established that 'pussyfooted around the main issue' (according to Joe Stettner), although some of them were actually very impressive climbs, particularly the Stettner brothers' own route, and Joe's solo route up the adjacent tower. However, the climbers were getting bolder; after World War II, the climbers were back. The Window route and Table Ledges opened by Tom Hornbein (of American Everest expedition fame) and others infringed ever so slightly on the Diamond – the name given to the top rock band, which takes the shape of a giant gem.

Although the Diamond is as much alpine big wall as pure rock, it is presently tackled as a single-day rock climbing task during the summer, hence its inclusion in this section.

As with many of the other harder routes, the opening ascents of this climb stretched over a period of several days, and sometimes weeks or even years. Once established, however, the climbs were much more easily completed, and generally in far faster times.

In 1952 Hornbein made the first of a series of serious exploratory forays out onto the vast Diamond itself, from various heights on both sides. These routes petered out, although some of his old ring pitons, which he left in place, were to puzzle later climbers who knew nothing of his 'sideways climbs'.

For quite a number of years, and for undisclosed reasons, the local rangers closed the Diamond to frustrated climbers. Then in 1960 they eventually relented, and issued permits to all the parties who had previously approached them. The first to respond were two Californians, David Rearick and Bob Camps. One of the requirements of the permit – so seriously did the Parks Service regard

the climb – was for two fully-equipped support parties to be available, one of which actually had to be stationed at the base of the route. The pair climbed in something of a 'siege' style; the first night they abseiled down to join their friends on the Broadway Ledge, the second night they bivouacked high on the face. The climb proved easier than anyone had ever imagined, requiring a bit of aid through some overhangs and past a thin crack system, and also involved climbing in a stream of icy cold falling water and past a few solid blocks of ice on the top pitches. Nonetheless, they took no falls, and found the route in a fairly straightforward way. This is not to make light of their efforts – it was a bold and difficult climb, completed in fine style by two tough and talented rock gymnasts. The opening of the Diamond was a serious dent in the concept of what was thought to be 'impossible'.

In true cowboy style, Rearick and Camps were fêted in a special Rodeo Parade held in Denver.

The Diamond, however, was not yet polished. Layton Kor then made a second ascent of the Rearick–Camps route, and decided that what was needed was a new direct route on the bottom wall to Broadway, and also a new route directly to the summit high point. In 1963, along with the young Tex Bossier (USA), Kor tackled the new route – a direct variation of his previous diagonal route. The pair climbed this route in a full-blown storm, with Bossier all the while doubting his chances of surviving 'with that lunatic' (Kor). They made it to Broadway in extreme conditions, and only just succeeded in traversing off. Bossier slipped, and tells the story of how he stopped by luck, right on the edge of the 600m (2000ft) drop of the lower wall. When he got to Kor, all they were belayed on was a single, loose knife-blade piton. 'If you'd kept going, we'd both have died,' was Kor's comment. The route was not repeated until 1975, and then it 'scared the ass off the climbers' (Michael Covington and Billy Westbay).

---- *Jack of Diamonds*   — *Forrest Solo*
— *Camps Route (Original)*   – – *Diagonal*

Opposite The sun illuminates the very impressive Diamond Face on Long's Peak, Rocky Mountain National Park, Colorado, USA.

Above A climber jumaring up fixed ropes on the Yellow Wall route on the Diamond, Long's Peak, Rocky Mountain National Park, Colorado, USA.

The first winter ascent took place in 1966, after Kor had returned from the disastrous Eiger Direct climb on which John Harlin had been killed. At first reluctant, he was persuaded to join Wayne Goss and Bob Culp (USA) in forging a new route. The trio climbed in high winds and sub-freezing temperatures, with their fingers succumbing to minor frostbite, and able to force only warm raspberry cooldrink down their ravaged throats.

In 1970 Bill Forrest, a schoolteacher, opened a new route (solo) up the Diamond, once again pushing the limits of the possible. 'Sometimes I have an irresistible desire to "find" myself through the solo experience. Being alone in the mountain crucible can lend a vital yet rational dimension to the sport. When soloing, the keen sensations experienced while climbing with a partner are intensified. Critical moves and decisions become super-exciting and meaningful. There is an absolute premium on the success of execution. Solo climbing demands the utmost in preparation.'

Top Steve Monks leading the sixth pitch on the first free ascent of Ozymandias Direct, Mount Buffalo – the strenuous but delicate nature of the climbing is apparent.

Above Steve Monks leading the second pitch of Ozymandias Direct. Finding suitable protection is both difficult and extremely taxing on a climber's resources.

OZYMANDIAS

The North Wall at Buffalo is reckoned to be one of Australia's most impressive cliffs. It offers long, test-piece routes on solid vertical granite, with awe-inspiring roofs running across the wall at two-thirds of its height on the Ozymandias sector.

In 1969 Chris Baxter and Chris Dewhirst tackled the route up the vast sweep of the North Wall. The rivalry to be the first was spirited, but the 'two Chrises' succeeded in beating the rest by means of bold climbing on marginal (insecure) placements, giving nail-biting aid climbing at Australian M6 (USA A4) – a serious grade, indicating the potential for long falls if the placements fail. It was an amazing line, and has become justifiably popular (although bolts now reduce the M6 to M4).

Another 'twin set' (this time real twins, not just in name), Geoff and Allan Gledhill, pioneered a more elegant direct finish. This route cut through the overhangs which had turned the 'Chrises' onto a series of traverses. By 1972, aid techniques and equipment had advanced sufficiently to allow the pair to move out into space and over the awe-inpiring overhang, to turn the roof at grade M4 – seemingly a less stringent grade than the 'Chrises' route, but in fact a more committing set of moves.

Above The North Wall at Mount Buffalo. Ozymandias Direct follows the corner and roof system.

The climbing community revelled in these and other aid climbs at Mount Buffalo. However, the pendulum was swinging to free climbing. 'Free' attempts were made on Ozymandias, but for over 17 years all were repulsed. Then came Steve Monks, an Englishman now resident in Australia. He and Jane Wilkinson laid siege to the route in the summer of 1989–90.

By now, serious training for climbing had crept in, as had new protection devices such as Friends, drilled expansion bolts, and 'sticky' rock boots. These advances, along with Steve's determination and fitness, helped him through the roofs at Grade 29 – a truly hard route.

Despite its climbing appeal and stunning setting, the route received no successful repeat attempts, until Steve himself repeated the bottom part of it in

1996–97 with Malcolm 'HB' Matheson. They then went on to free the Direct variation, graded as 28, with the pitch through the roof regarded as one of the most impressive free climbs ever done.

The advent of sport climbing has temporarily turned the attention away from these natural-gear and aid routes. Ozymandias itself finally received its second full free ascent in 1998, and at the time of writing, Ozymandias Direct still awaits a repeat free attempt. Neither route has yet been done on-sight. Whoever succeeds in that will be carving their names firmly into the history of one of Australia's most challenging and charismatic climbs.

— *Ozymandias (Original)*   ···· *Ozymandias Direct*

Below A bivouac on Ozymandias. A one-day ascent remains as a challenge to future climbers.

Below The leader's viewpoint – looking down Ozymandias' superbly textured and coloured rock.

THE BARD

In Australia's western Victorian plains, out of the flatness of the wheatfields a huge mass of rock appears. This is Mount Arapiles (Djurid, to use the Aboriginal name) – one of the climbing paradises of Australia, a cliff of hard quartzite sandstone.

Because of its isolation (the nearest large city, Melbourne, is over 300km, or 180 miles, away) it only attracted the attention of rock climbers in the early 1960s. Two pioneers were Jim Newlands and Bruce Hocking, who keenly eyed the line of cracks and slabs which ran up the highest central part of the cliff, now called the Bard Buttress.

With hardly any equipment, climbing with the rope tied around their waist (the only way in the pre-harness period), and in the rigid walking boots and sandshoes common to the day, Newlands and Hocking alternately climbed the almost protectionless 35m (120ft) lower slab in a number of

Left Louise Shepherd leading the fifth pitch of the classic Bard, Mount Arapiles, Victoria.

Above Shepherd completing the crux move onto the small overhanging nose.

short pitches, moving on to the start of the crux pitches. Newlands led the key hand-traverse under an overhang in a rush, climbing through it onto an airy stance on a projecting nose. They then tackled an improbable-looking blank wall, which necessitated delicate traversing until a bottomless chimney was reached. This entire 60m (200ft) section was led with minimal protection.

The name 'Bard' arose from Jim's quote from Shakespeare's Hamlet, 'Oh that too too solid flesh would melt'. (Jim said it was a result of his 'portly shape' and a wish to be lighter for the hand traverse.)

Bard remains one of the most popular routes in the country – for its (now) relatively easy grade, it offers a superb climbing experience in a unique and charismatic area. The lack of good protection on some pitches, as well as the tricky footwork, still make this a route to be reckoned with. It is indeed a piece of 'living history', where one can easily imagine echoes of the earlier climbers (and, of course, the great Bard's words) rebounding off the orange-red rock, urging you on until you sit on the top, in quiet contemplation.

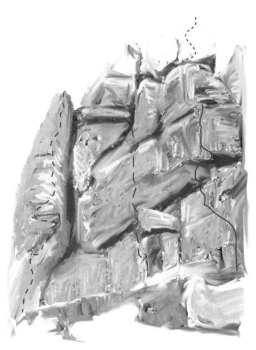

——— *Resignation*
— — *The Good, the Bad and the Ugly*
- - - *The Bard*
····· *Quo Vadis*

Right Kay Audenart lugging a huge rack of protection up Chinese Algebra, Mount Arapiles, Victoria.

ROCK CLIMBS ELSEWHERE

Excellent pure rock climbs can be found in many corners of the world: Australia, South and Central Africa, South America, Europe and the East, to name but a few key areas. It would need another whole series of volumes to do these justice, and years of debate and consultation to decide on which to include. Here are pictures of a few to excite the mind, and incite the visit.

Above Mike Cartwright on Sorcery (Grade 27) at the Restaurant at the End of the Universe crag, Waterval Boven, South Africa.

Right Simon Mentz and Brad Arnold on the second pitch of Fringe Dweller on Mount Rosea in the Grampians, Victoria, Australia.

Top Sunset over Table Bay, Cape Town, South Africa, as Todd Skinner climbs through the final moves of a huge roof on Table Mountain.

Above Volker Jurisch abseiling off The Moai, a dolerite column at Fortescue Bay, Tasman Peninsula, one of Tasmania's many superb sea stacks.

Left A climber searching for the right piece of protection gear on Dicer's Groove, The Cobbler, Southern Highlands, Scotland.

Clockwise from top left Immaculate dolomite on the Vinci Route, South Ridge Direct, Pizzo Cengalo in the Bregaglia Alps; Andrew de Klerk jumaring on Milner Peak, Western Cape, South Africa; Tom Rangitich climbs in a more modern, lightweight, fast style – De blioff Proffondicum, Verdon, France; Salli O'Connor on the final pitches of the long, full-day route Epereon Sublime, Verdon Gorge, France.

THE ROCK GYMNASTS

The challenge of the vertical can be long and arduous, such as on the 8000m peaks or alpine routes, or it can be extremely short and yet still arduous. In the world of sport climbing, the dedicated, limit-pushing climber strives to complete the 'hardest' route possible, irrespective of whether it is 4m (13ft) or 40m (130ft) long. A 100m (300ft) race is no less taxing than a 10,000m (6-mile) race, though it requires a totally different commitment. In the same way, sport climbing should be viewed as neither a lesser nor greater form of the art of climbing.

The essence of sport climbing lies in the preprepared nature of the route. A sport route is a route which has fixed protection — that is, the points into which the climber clips him- or herself are permanent structures, preplaced in the rock. The only protection equipment other than the rope usually consists of quickdraws — two carabiners joined by a short sling which are clipped into the in-situ protection.

In contrast to most other forms of climbing, in sport climbing it is considered quite normal to fall off a route repeatedly while preparing to complete the route from bottom to top. Falling and repeating moves, resting on tight rope, pulling on quickdraws during practice attempts, practising sequences of moves, inspecting the route on abseil or top-rope, watching others climb the route, asking for information, watching videos of the route, and even in extreme cases building 'models' of the route in one's training cellar — all of these are legitimate sport-climbing techniques.

Sport climbing is the most rapidly growing branch of climbing. Sport crags are usually easy to access, with no long walk-ins; the equipment required is less costly than a large traditional gear rack; it has a 'fun' element which appeals particularly to the younger generation; the competitive element is more visible; and the number of routes completed is generally greater and hence more satisfying in the modern, pressurized world. It is inherently safer in that the protection places are solid and reliable. It also relates more directly to competition climbing, and hence to media hype, prizes, and climbing 'big time'.

SPORT CLIMBING ON THE HARD SANDSTONE OF THE WESTERN CAPE, SOUTH AFRICA, WITH THE WIDE EXPANSE OF FALSE BAY IN THE BACKGROUND.

Sport Climbing

The Vertical Arena

Most countries around the world boast sport routes. The Mecca of sport climbing, however, is still France, with its thousands of routes in all grades and ranging in length from 3m (10ft) to 300m (1000ft) or longer.

The routes chosen for this section comprise two historically significant sport climbs which have both remained unrepeated for years. Although it might seem unfair to compare the first ascent of a 20m (70ft) sport route on a roadside crag with the efforts of the first team up Everest, the absolute commitment to intensive training, and the number of repeated attempts on the route, should leave one with no doubt as to the difficulties involved. Both routes in this section have been Redpoint ascents (*see* page 155).

ACTION DIRECTE

Wolfgang Güllich was the 'Wunderkind' of German (and in fact European) climbing when on 11 September 1991 he completed the incredibly hard 12m (30ft) of 45-degree overhanging limestone in Frankenjura, Germany, that he named Action Directe after the French Terrorist group, 'because it was an attack on your fingers'. For two years, Güllich worked out specifically for this one route, concentrating on improving his already immense finger strength to cope with its 'monos' – holds which can only accommodate a single finger. He then worked on the route for 11 days, over a period of 10 weeks, linking the difficult pieces bit by bit, until he decided that he felt ready, and then climbed it flawlessly in just 70 seconds. Shortly after he had completed this milestone route, he worked as stunt double for Sylvester Stallone in the film *Cliffhanger*, doing the unbe-

lievably hard climbing sequences below the awesome roof in the Italian Dolomites – the opening shots of the film. He never saw the final product of the film, as sadly, after an early morning radio interview in August 1992, he apparently fell asleep at the wheel of his car and had a fatal accident. The climbing world was deprived of one of its brightest young stars.

The route remained unrepeated, with many climbers reluctant even to attempt it, leaving it a fitting tribute to Güllich. The closest near-repeat came in 1992 when Ben Moon, then rated as the most powerful climber in the UK, after seven days of practice on the steep prow of rock, was convinced that his next attempt would be 'the one'. After a flowing ascent to a scant metre from the top, he pulled a tendon, and was out of the game. The second ascent was made soon after Ben Moon's attempt by Alexander Adler.

The psychological, and physical, barrier of 9a gave this route almost mythical appeal, and it is still spoken of in hushed tones.

With his many first ascents, including Action Directe, Wall Street and Punks in the Gym, Güllich repeatedly pushed the frontiers of hard sport climbing. His other firsts include a free solo ascent of the spectacular Separate Reality in Yosemite Valley, USA – a feat that demanded the cool head and extreme fitness for which he was famous. His ascents of Eternal Flame on the Trango Towers and Riders in the Storm on the Towers of Paine placed Güllich at the cutting edge of big wall climbing, proving that he was a true master in many diverse branches of the sport. Wolfgang Güllich was beyond doubt one of the most influential climbers of the 80s and early 90s.

Opposite Weisse Rose, a taxing sport climb that demands absolute fitness and total commitment.
Top left Dramatic falls onto the solid protection of bolt anchors are commonplace in sport climbing.
Bottom left Wolfgang Güllich on Action Directe, showing his incredible power with one-finger holds.

OPEN AIR

The south-facing rocks of the Schleier Wasser-fallen area near Kitzbühel in Austria boast few 'easy' routes – only 18 below Grade 6C+. It is the avowed aim of the 'local boy' Alex Huber to make this one of Europe's hardest climbing areas. With a cliff that overhangs some 25m (75ft) in 50m (150ft) of height, that should not be too diffi-cult a task! Already a large number of climbs over the awe-inspiring grade of 8b exist, all Huber cre-ations. His hardest route is undoubtedly Open Air, at Grade 9a (5.14d). The route certainly leaves plenty of air open under the climber's feet, with

not a single real resting spot in its 50m (150ft) of overhanging effort – an unusual length for a high-grade sport-climbing route.

It starts with 20m (70ft) of Grade 8 overhang, then 'relaxes' into 15m (50ft) of high Grade 7 at 45 degrees, leading to a sloping ledge for the 'rest' before the crux. The route then turns on the energy, with a further 15m (50ft) of pinch grips, thin slopers, side and underclings (see page 159), single-finger pockets and constant overhang.

The route did not come easily – it took months of preparation before Huber managed his first full Redpoint. Open Air is now one of the most

sought-after repeats in the sport-climbing world. Huber does not limit himself to sport climbs. He has been active, with his brother Thomas, in cutting-edge routes in major mountains all over the world, from the big walls of Yosemite and the European Alps to superalpine ascents of Himalayan big walls – he is a true mountaineer.

Below Wolfgang Güllich on his magnificent first ascent of the finger-tendon-wrecking Action Directe – this difficult route has only had one successful repeat climb.

TYPES OF ASCENT

On-sight Flash

This is considered by most sport climbers to be the best style. The climber walks up to a route, and leads it from bottom to top on the first attempt, with no falls or any pre-knowledge of the route.

Redpoint

The climber has practised the route any number of times, and worked out the critical holds and sequences bit by bit. The Redpoint is obtained when the climber finally leads the route from bottom to top with no falls or rests. Redpoint ascents are considered normal for the harder grades.

Top Alex Huber clings tenaciously to the tiny holds on the crux section of Gambit (Grade 8c+), one of his desperately hard sport routes at Schleier Wasserfallen in Austria. This particular route has seen very few repeats.

Right A complex and energy-draining set of moves are required to overcome the wildly overhanging middle section of Black Power (Grade 8c+), yet another 'top of the difficulty range' Huber creation at Schleier Wasserfallen.

THE 8000M PEAKS

Everest	Nepal	8848m (29,028ft)
K2	Karakoram	8611m (28,253ft)
Kangchenjunga	Sikkim	8586m (28,170ft)
Lhotse	Nepal	8516m (27,940ft)
Makalu	Nepal	8463m (27,767ft)
Cho Oyu	Nepal	8201m (26,907ft)
Dhaulagiri	Nepal	8167m (26,795ft)
Manaslu	Nepal	8163m (26,782ft)
Nanga Parbat	Punjab	8125m (26,656ft)
Annapurna	Nepal	8091m (26,545ft)
Gasherbrum I	Karakoram	8068m (26,471ft)
Broad Peak	Karakoram	8047m (26,402ft)
Shisha Pangma	Nepal	8046m (26,398ft)
Gasherbrum II	Karakoram	8035m (26,362ft)

GRADES

Grading systems vary widely. Alpine routes are usually graded from F (facile – easy) to ED (extrèmement difficile – very hard), or from Alpine Grade I to VI. Rock climbs have many different although comparable grades (e.g. USA 5.14c = UK 7c/E9 = Australian 34 = UIAA XI = very, very hard!). Ice climbing has its own set of grades, such as WI5 (water ice at Grade 5) or M8+ (mixed ice at 8+, currently a very hard grade). Aid climbing ranges from A1 (easy) to A5 (desperate). 'Mixed' routes, such as those on Fitzroy or Cerro Torre, are thus rated VI / 5.11 / A4 (hard alpine, including ice, rock and aid). It is usual not to apply these grades to major Himalayan-scale climbs, which often defy conventional grading systems.

BIBLIOGRAPHY

BENUZZI, FELICE *No Picnic on Mount Kenya*, William Kimber, London 1952

BLUM, ARLENE *Annapurna – A Woman's Place*, Granada, London 1984

BONATTI, WALTER *On the Heights*, Hart-Davis, London 1964

BONINGTON, CHRIS (Ed) *Great Climbs*, Mitchell Beazley, London 1995

BONINGTON, CHRIS *Quest for Adventure*, Hodder and Stoughton, London 1981

CANNING, JOHN (Ed) *50 Great Journeys*, Hamlyn Publishing Group, UK 1968

CAPPON, MASSIMO *Rock and Ice Climbing*, Orbis Publishing Ltd, London 1983

CHAMOUX, BENOIT *Everest, Minus 2 Metres*, Initiative 1993

CLARKE, CHARLES *Epic Adventures: Everest*, Sackett and Marshall, London 1978

CLEARE, JOHN *Mountains*, MacMillan, London 1975

DEARDEN, PAUL *Classic Rock Climbs*, Blandford, London 1994

DUMLER, H; BURKHARDT, W *The High Mountain of the Alps: 4000m Peaks*, Diadem Books, London; The Mountaineers, Seattle 1993

GILLMAN, PETER (Ed) *Everest – the Best Writing and Pictures from Seventy Years of Human Endeavour*, Peter Gillman Ltd, London 1993

GODDARD, DALE; NEUMANN, UDO *Performance Rock Climbing*, Stackpole Books, Mechanicsberg 1993

HARRER, HEINRICH *The White Spider*, Hart-Davis, London 1959

HATTINGH, GARTH *The Climber's Handbook*, New Holland, London 1998

HEPP, TILMAN *Wolfgang Güllich, Leben in der Senkrechten*, Rosenheimer, Rosenheim 1993

HERZOG, MAURICE *Annapurna: Conquest of the First 8000m Peak*, Alden Press, Oxford 1953

HORNBEIN, THOMAS *Everest, the West Ridge*, George Allen & Unwin, London 1971

KEARNEY, ALAN *Mountaineering in Patagonia*, Cloudcap, Seattle 1993

KEENLYSIDE, FRANCIS *Peaks and Pioneers – The Story of Mountaineering*, Paul Eck 1975

MESSNER, REINHOLD *The Big Walls*, Kaye and Ward, London 1978

MESSNER, REINHOLD *K2, Mountain of Mountains*, Kaye and Ward, London 1981

MOUNTAINEERS, THE *Mountaineering, The Freedom of the Hills*, 5th Edition, The Mountaineers, Washington 1992.

NOYCE, W; McMORRIN, I *World Atlas of Mountaineering*, Nelson, London 1969

PATEY, TOM *One Man's Mountains*, Gollancz 1971

PERRIN, JIM (Ed) *Mirrors in the Cliffs*, Diadem, London 1983

RÉBUFFAT, GASTON *The Mont Blanc Massif, the 100 Finest Routes*, Kaye and Ward, London 1975

ROWELL, GALEN *The Vertical World of Yosemite*, Wilderness Press, California 1974

SCOTT, DOUG *Himalayan Climber*, Diadem Books, London 1992

SHIPTON, ERIC *Blank on the Map*, Hodder and Stoughton, London 1938

TAPLIN, THOMAS *Aconcagua, The Stone Sentinel*, Eli Ely 1953

TASKER, JOE *Everest the Cruel Way*, Eyre Methuen, London 1981

TRUFFER, BEAT *The History of the Matterhorn*, NBV, Amsterdam 1992

UNSWORTH, WALT *This Climbing Game*, Penguin, London 1985

UNSWORTH, WALT *The Encyclopaedia of Mountaineering*, Hodder and Stoughton, London 1992

VON KANEL, JURG *Schweiz Plaisir*, Filidor, Reichenbach 1992

WILLIAMS, PAUL *Rock Climbing in Snowdonia*, Constable, London 1990

WILSON, KEN *Classic Rock*, Hart Davis MacGibbon, London 1978

Journals and Magazines

Various short articles and general information from:
Climber Magazine (Glasgow, UK)
Climbing Magazine (Aspen, USA)
High Magazine (Sheffield, UK)
Journal of the Mountain Club of South Africa
Mountain Magazine (London, UK)
Roktpunkt (Germany)
The American Alpine Club Journal

Abseil – A means of descending a rope safely, the speed being controlled by friction of rope around the body or via an abseil device.

Acclimatization – The progressive adaptation of the human body to the rarified air at high altitudes.

Aid climbing – Climbing that relies on the use of pegs, nuts, ACDs (Active Camming Devices) and other protection equipment for upward progression.

Alpine climbing (Alpinism) – Climbing which traditionally implies glacier or snow travel, higher mountains and the ascent of a peak; usually alpine ascents necessitate self-sufficiency of the climbers, and speed in climbing.

Alpine style – Alpine climbing as applied to the great mountain ranges, in which the route is ascended in one push, without fixed ropes and numerous heavily stocked sub-camps.

Altitude sickness – The result of bad acclimatization; can result in death. Otherwise known as AMS (Acute Mountain Sickness).

Amphitheatre – A large 'bowl' of rock, usually associated with steep rock faces.

Anchor – A point of attachment of ropes or slings to rock; can be natural (rock spike or flake, or a tree) or placed (a bolt, peg or nut).

Arête – A narrow ridge of rock, ice or snow. On a smaller cliff, this describes a steep, narrow rock ridge.

Belay – The system used to stop a fall by using a rope; includes the anchor, the belayer and the belay devices or method. To belay means to hold the rope in such a way as to be able to arrest a fall.

Bergschrund – The final big crevasse at the head of a glacier, usually where the rock wall begins or the ice face steepens.

Big walls – Long, technically demanding routes usually needing many days for ascent. Not every pitch need be climbed by each climber; mechanical ascenders are often used by the second climber to follow the leader.

Bivouac – To spend the night in the open on a route or mountain. May be a forced bivouac if this is unintentional.

Bolt – A metal expansion bolt, glued or fastened into a predrilled hole in the rock face; used for belays or running protection.

Bouldering – Unroped climbing on any small rock face or surface, including walls and buildings.

Camming device – A protection device with metal cams which expand and bite harder into the rock under load, often called ACDs (Active Camming Devices), e.g. a Friend or Camalot.

Carabiner (crab) – Metal snap-ring which can open on one side (the gate), used to attach protection to slings or ropes, or for general use in climbing where a device which opens is needed; locking carabiners are fitted with sleeves to prevent accidental opening.

Ceiling – A 'roof' or large horizontal overhang.

Chalk – Powder used to dry sweat from hands; usually a form of magnesium carbonate with other substances such as silica.

Chimneying – Climbing a fissure or chimney by using back-and-foot or similar techniques against opposite walls.

Classic route – A climb with a reputation of being outstanding, as a result of location, history, elegance and other often indefinable associations. It can be of any grade.

Committing – A route or move where retreat would be difficult or impossible.

Cornice – An overhanging mass of snow on a ridge formed by wind on newly deposited snow.

Couloir – A broad gully.

Crag – A smallish outcrop of rock, usually with routes of only one or two pitches.

Crampons – Metal frames with down- and front-pointing spikes, fitted to mountain boots to assist passage on hard snow or ice.

Crevasse – A huge split in a glacier, frequently hidden under overlying snow cover.

Crux – The most difficult section or move of a climb.

Descendeur – A device used to increase friction and yet allow the rope to move during an abseil.

Dièdre (Dihedral) – A corner on a rock wall or face, often referred to as an 'open book'.

Diretissima – The most direct route possible; the path of a falling drop of water.

Gear – General name for climbing equipment, but usually used more specifically to refer to protection equipment.

Glissade – To slide down snow slopes without skis; climbers do this standing in their boots.

Gneiss – A type of rock, characterized by a loose, grainy texture.

Grade – Difficulty rating given to a climb by consensus of climbers.

Ice screw – Metal screw that is hammered or screwed into the ice to give running protection or a belay anchor.

Icefall – A frozen waterfall.

Jumar – The original make of ascender, a metal toothed device which clamps onto the rope and has since given its name to the technique of ascending ropes by means of similar ascenders.

Layback – Method of ascending a crack or edge where the hands grip and pull while the feet provide opposing counterforce.

Marginal – A runner or aid point with an uncertain degree of security to hold a fall or pressure.

Mixed route – A route involving both rock and snow/ice climbing.

Natural-gear protection – Protection which is placed by the leader and removed by the second, e.g. nuts and camming devices (not preplaced bolts or pegs).

Niche – A recess in a rock face.

Nose – A protruding mass of rock, varying from tiny (on a crag) to huge (on a large mountain).

Nut – A metal wedge or chock designed for protection in cracks.

Objective danger – Occurrences outside of the control of the climber, such as stone fall, avalanche, lightning.

Off-width – A crack too small to accommodate the body, but too large to allow for a hand- or foot jam. Usually very tricky to climb.

On-sight – To lead a climb flawlessly the first time, with no preknowledge of the route or moves.

Pitch – A section of rock/snow/ice which is climbed between major belay points; often a pitch stops at a suitable stance or anchor point.

Piton (peg or pin) – Metal spike with an attachment eye for a carabiner; it is hammered into crevices for use as protection.

Portaledge – A collapsible, reinforced stretcher which is hung from protection on a big wall, allowing climbers to work or sleep; often used as a belay ledge.

Protection – Nylon slings or metal devices (e.g. nuts, chocks, hexes, stoppers and ACDs) fixed into the rock; used to stop climbers from falling too far, or to anchor climbers or rope to belay points.

Prussik (prussic) – Using short lengths of thin cord specially tied into loops and wound around the rope in a set fashion as a sliding friction knot to ascend the rope.

Redpointing – A climbing style (in sport climbing) where any amount and form of practice and preparation of the route is allowed, providing the climb is finally led without pulling or resting on the protection points.

Rock boots – Lightweight, specialized, tight-fitting boots with sticky high-friction rubber soles.

Rognon – A rock 'island' in a glacier; a safe resting place or hut site.

Roof – An overhang which sticks out horizontally.

Route – A 'pathway' up the mountain; this can be a recognized, written-up description, or a new route over unknown ground, previously never ascended.

Sérac – A block of ice in an ice fall; potentially hazardous, as these periodically break off.

Slab – A large, off-vertical, often featureless sheet of rock; best climbed with balance techniques.

Solo climbing – To climb alone; soloing without a rope is called 'free soloing'.

Spindrift – Loose powder snow blowing or falling down.

Sustained route – A route with a continuous high level of difficulty.

Technical – Referring to climbing where the moves are complex and difficult, requiring skill, thought and technique.

Technique ('good') – An effective method of overcoming the climbing problem using minimal effort and energy.

Top-rope – To climb a pitch without leading it: the rope is attached from above.

Topo – A semipictorial diagram to illustrate the line of a route.

Underclings – Using the hand in a palm-up position to hold onto an edge or protrusion.

Verglassed – Usually applied to rock which is covered by a thin, almost invisible layer of clear ice which makes climbing more difficult. Thick verglass is akin to water ice, and can be climbed as such.

Voie normale – The usual route up a mountain.

Wall – Large, steep mountain face.

Water ice – Hard, brittle ice formed by the freezing of water, as opposed to snow compaction; often blue or clear.

Wind chill (factor) – The effect of the wind in dissipating heat from a body; this lowers the effective temperature below the actual still air temperature.

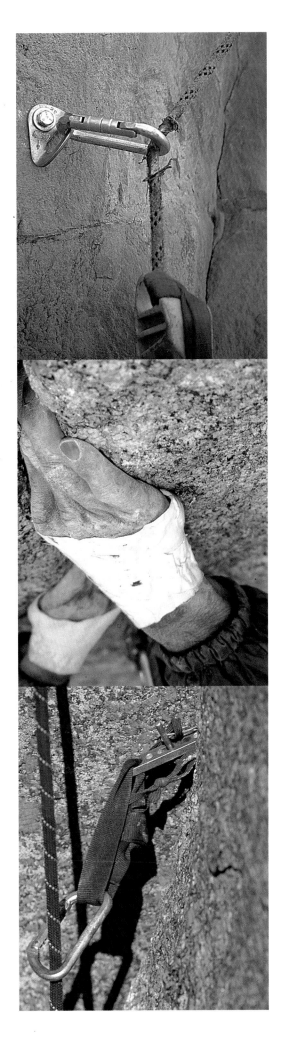

ACKNOWLEDGEMENTS

I would like to thank many colleagues, too numerous to mention, for good times in the mountains and for help with this book. They will know who they are! Special thanks are due to: Leonard Rust, in particular for his assistance with the sport climbing section and captions; Greg Pritchard for the information from 'down under' in Australia; Eric Penman for proofreading and advice; Vivian Solomons and the Mountain Club of South Africa for the use of the library (as well as for the joys of membership), and to Lynnette, Garrick and Dylan for support and sanity when things threatened to get out of control! Lastly to Thea, the long-suffering editor, and Peter, the designer — thank you for your help, patience and sound advice.

The copyright © of the photographs rests with the following photographers and / or their agents:

CBL = *Chris Bonington Library;* **HH** = *Hedgehog House;* **MC** = *Mountain Camera;*
RGS = *Royal Geographical Society;* **SIL** = *Struik Image Library.*

Bill Atkinson (HH): *p 84 (top);* **Daryl Balfour (SIL):** *p 70;* **Pat Barrett (HH):** *p 118;* **Dries Bekker:** *pp 36, 65, 84 (bottom right);* **Peter Boardman (CBL):** *p 22 (centre);* **Chris Bonington (CBL):** *pp 27 (bottom), 28 (bottom right), 34, 38 (top), 39 (bottom), 52, 54/55, 57, 58 (centre), 60 (top), 60/61, 78, 92, 93 (top left, bottom), 96;* **Chris Brasher (MC):** *p 26 (right);* **Gottlieb Braun-Elwert (HH):** *pp 100 (bottom), 117;* **Ulf Carlsson:** *pp 56, 62, 63 (top, bottom), 64 (bottom left), 74;* **Simon Carter:** *pp 15 (centre), 124/125, 144 (top left, top centre, top right, bottom left, bottom centre, bottom right), 145 (top), 146 (left, right), 147, 148 (right), 149 (bottom right);* **Graham Charles (HH):** *p 3;* **Ska Cilliers:** *back cover (centre right), pp 35 (top), 112 (top);* **Lionel Clay (HH):** *endpapers (left, right), p 158 (bottom);* **John Cleare (MC):** *cover (spine), pp 12 (centre, right), 15 (left, right), 16 (right), 25 (top right), 28 (bottom left), 71 (top, centre), 80 (top, centre), 87 (top, bottom), 88/89, 90 (top, bottom), 91, 94/95, 128 (centre), 130 (bottom), 135 (top left, bottom left), 136;* **Julie-Ann Clyma / R Payne:** *pp 1, 17 (right), 67, 88;* **Peter Cole:** *pp 45, 66 (top, bottom), 69 (bottom), 143;* **Arthur Collins (HH):** *p 60 (bottom);* **Guy Cotter (HH):** *front cover, pp 32 (top left, top centre, top right), 33;* **Nick Cradock (HH):** *pp 116/117;* **Chris Craggs (MC):** *pp 7 (top), 126, 158 (top);* **Chris Curry (HH):** *pp 64 (top), 69 (top);* **Dave Davies:** *p 97 (top, bottom);* **Leo Dickinson (CBL):** *pp 22 (bottom), 53;* **Kurt Diemberger:** *pp 44 (top), 49 (top, centre, bottom);* **Grant Dixon:** *back cover (bottom right), pp 13, 21, 23, 30/31 (top), 41, 42/43;* **Grant Dixon (HH):** *p 100 (top, centre);* **Steve Eggington:** *pp 14, 72 (centre);* **Duncan Elliott:** *pp 7 (centre), 104/105;* **Edmund February:** *pp 16 (left), 112 (bottom), 113 (top, bottom), 150 (top right), 160 (top);* **G I Finch (RGS):** *p 25 (bottom left);* **Julian Fisher:** *p 119 (right);* **Mike Freeman (HH):** *p 103;* **Stewart Green:** *back cover (top centre, centre left), pp 6, 133 (centre), 134, 138 (left), 138/139, 139 (top right, bottom right), 140, 141 (bottom left), 142;* **Nick Groves (HH):** *pp 4/5;* **Andy Hackland:** *back cover (top left, bottom left), pp 40 (top), 42 (left), 47, 72 (top), 79, 151;* **Hall and Ball Archive (HH):** *pp 12 (left), 38 (bottom), 44 (bottom);* **Jim Harding (HH):** *pp 109, 110;* **Bill Hatcher:** *pp 7 (bottom), 17 (left), 108 (top, centre, bottom), 149 (top right), 152 (top);* **Gerhard Heidorn:** *pp 152 (bottom), 154;* **Fran Hunziker:** *back cover (top right), pp 127, 133 (top, bottom), 135 (right), 148 (left);* **André Joubert:** *p 106;* **Tadashi Kajiyama (MC):** *pp 48, 50, 51;* **Chris Lomax:** *p 130 (top);* **MC:** *p 24 (top right, bottom);* **Bobby Model:** *pp 8/9, 46, 107, 129, 150 (bottom right), 160 (centre, bottom);* **Jerry Moffat:** *p 137;* **Colin Monteath (HH):** *pp 73, 101;* **Colin Monteath (MC):** *pp 27 (top), 32 (bottom), 115;* **Jason Nelson (© 1998 Jason Nelson, All Rights Reserved):** *p 141 (top right);* **Hennie Niemand:** *p 64 (bottom right);* **Bill O'Connor (MC):** *p 150 (bottom left);* **Cathy O'Dowd:** *pp 18/19, 28 (top);* **Darryn Pegram (HH):** *p 37;* **Tom Prentice:** *back cover (bottom centre), pp 35 (bottom), 72 (bottom), 75, 80 (bottom), 82, 83, 84 (bottom left), 85, 98/99 (top), 128 (top), 131 (left, right), 149 (left), 150 (top left);* **Steve Razzetti (RGS):** *p 20;* **RGS:** *pp 22 (top), 26 (left);* **Peter Ribton:** *pp 98 (bottom), 99 (bottom), 132;* **Paul Rogers (HH):** *pp 40 (bottom), 128 (bottom);* **Kevin Schaefer (HH):** *p 86;* **Doug Scott:** *p 90 (centre);* **Doug Scott (CBL):** *pp 30 (bottom), 58 (top, bottom);* **Mike Scott:** *pp 31 (bottom), 71 (bottom), 93 (top right), 119 (left), 123;* **Howard Smith:** *back cover (centre), pp 81, 84 (bottom centre), 156/157;* **Kevin Smith:** *p 111;* **T H Somervell (RGS):** *p 24 (top left);* **Geoff Spearpoint (HH):** *p 59;* **Alastair Stevenson (MC):** *p 68;* **Mark Synnott:** *pp 120, 121 (top, centre, bottom), 122 (left, right);* **Peter Taw (HH):** *p 39 (top right);* **Luke Trihey (HH):** *p 145 (bottom left, bottom right);* **Hugh van Noorden (HH):** *pp 29, 76/77;* **Beth Wald:** *p 114 (top, centre, bottom);* **Geoff Wayatt (HH):** *p 102;* **Heinz Zak:** *pp 2, 153, 155 (left, right).*